Donald R. Wood

Grace and Holy Trinity

Cathedral

Kansas City, Missouri

1962

THERE IS A SMALL-TYPE EDITION OF THIS
BOOK, DIARY SIZE, IN CLOTH 4s. 6d. NET

First published	November 1925
Second Edition	March 1926
hird Edition	November 1926
rth and Revised Edition	January 1928
Edition	April 1929
Edition	January 1930
h Edition	December 1930
th Edition (large type)	January 1931
th Edition	April 1932
enth Edition	November 1933
Eleventh Edition	April 1937
Twelfth Edition	June 1942
Thirteenth Edition . . .	January 1944
Fourteenth Edition . . .	October 1945
Fifteenth Edition . . .	October 1946
Sixteenth Edition (large type)	March 1947
Seventeenth Edition . . .	September 1949
Eighteenth Edition (large type)	March 1954

(completing 59,000 copies)

Reprinted by lithography in Great Britain by
Jarrold & Sons, Ltd., Norwich

247.6
021

7805093

A DEVOTIONAL DIARY

ARRANGED BY

J. H. OLDHAM

S.C.M. PRESS LTD.

58 BLOOMSBURY STREET, LONDON, W.C.1.

INTRODUCTION

Two years ago I published a small Devotional Diary for which there has been a sufficient demand to justify the publication of a new edition. In its present form the Diary has been enlarged to nearly twice its former size, and entirely rewritten, though a considerable portion of the old material has been retained.

The distinctive feature of the Diary is the provision for record of the time spent in quiet each day. I know that some of those who have expressed appreciation of the suggestions for meditation have no use for this kind of spiritual account keeping. But others, like myself, have found it an aid against self-deception.

In addition to the pages for record there are a few blank pages for noting subjects for prayer.

A much better book could have been prepared by someone with greater opportunities for wider reading than I have had. I have been largely limited in my choice of quotations to the comparatively few books which, in the midst of a life given to practical affairs, I have found time to read during the last three or four years, supplemented by suggestions from a few anthologies. I should hesitate to offer to the public something which falls so far short of the ideal, were it not that the reception accorded to the first edition encourages me to believe that thoughts which have been illuminating and strengthening to myself may be of some help to others.

I have tried so far as possible to verify the original references. The source of the quotation when known is given in the index at the end. The sign (X) indicates either that the passage so marked could not be traced or that I have expressed in my own words a thought suggested by a passage which did not readily lend itself to direct quotation.

Cordial acknowledgment is made to the following authors and publishers who have kindly given permission to make quotations from the works named :

Professor John Baillie for quotations from *The Roots of Religion in the Human Soul* (Hodder & Stoughton);

Introduction

Professor William Adams Brown for two prayers and two verses from *The Quiet Hour* (The Association Press);

Mr. John Buchan for a quotation from "The Strong Man Armed" in *Poems Scots and English* (Thomas Nelson & Sons);

Messrs. Burns, Oates & Washbourne for quotations from "A Judgment of Heaven" and "The Hound of Heaven" by Francis Thompson;

Messrs. Jonathan Cape and Mr. Middleton Murry for a number of quotations from *The Life of Jesus*;

Messrs. Chatto & Windus and the Executors of the late George Macdonald for the poem "That Holy Thing";

Messrs. Chatto & Windus and Messrs. Charles Scribner's Sons for a prayer from *Vailima Papers* by R. L. Stevenson;

Messrs. J. M. Dent & Sons, and the Executors of the late Baron von Hügel, for permission to quote freely from *The Mystical Element in Religion*, from the two volumes of *Essays and Addresses*, and from *Selected Letters*;

Messrs. Doubleday, Doubleday, Page & Co., and Mr. Edwin Markham for a quotation from the poem "Revelation" in *Collected Poems*, 1927;

Messrs. Duckworth & Co. for a quotation from the poem "Kindness" by T. Sturge Moore;

Messrs. Elkin Mathews & Marrot and Mr. Laurence Binyon for a quotation from *The Secret*;

Messrs. W. Heffer & Sons and Mr. J. S. Hoyland for permission to quote freely from *The Sacrament of Common Life and The Fourfold Sacrament*;

Professor A. G. Hogg for a quotation from *A Morning Meditation*;

Messrs. John Lane & Co. for lines from Mr. Stephen Phillips' poems "Grief and God" and "The Poet's Prayer";

Messrs. Little, Little, Brown & Co. and Mr. Edward Everett Hale for a quotation from the poem "The Nameless Saints";

Messrs. Longmans, Green & Co. for several quotations from William James's *Varieties of Religious Experience*;

The Macmillan Company and Professor E. F. Scott for permission to quote freely from *The Ethical Teaching of Jesus*;

Messrs. Macmillan and Mr. Rudyard Kipling for quotations from "If" and "The Children's Song" in *Songs from Books*;

Messrs. Macmillan and Canon B. H. Streeter for several quotations from *Reality*;

Messrs. Macmillan and Dr. A. S. Way for several quotations from *The Letters of St. Paul* (sixth edition);

Messrs. Methuen and Mr. Rudyard Kipling for a quotation from "The Explorer" in *The Five Nations*;

Introduction

The Estate of Mr. T. B. Mosher for two verses of the hymn
" Glad that I live am I " by Lizette Woodworth Reese;
Sir Henry Newbolt for quotations from the poems " Sailing
at Dawn " and " Clifton Chapel " in *Poems New and
Old*, and also from " Our Lady " by Mary Coleridge;
The Oxford University Press and the Egyptian Exploration
Society for four passages from *The New Sayings of Jesus*,
from Oxyrhynchus;
Mr. Cecil Palmer and Mr. G. K. Chesterton for a quotation
from " The House of Christmas " in *Collected Poems;*
Messrs. Sidgwick & Jackson and Mr. John Drinkwater for
the quotation from " A Prayer " in *Collected Poems ;*
Messrs. Sidgwick & Jackson and Mr. John Masefield for two
quotations from *The Everlasting Mercy ;*
Mr. L. Pearsall Smith for a quotation from *Trivia ;*
Professor W. R. Sorley for two verses from " Expectans
Expectavi " in *Marlborough and other Poems* by C. H.
Sorley;
The Editor of the *Spectator* for verses from a poem which
appeared in its columns;
Lady Spring-Rice for a quotation from the poem " The
Two Fatherlands " by Sir Cecil Spring-Rice;
The Yale University Press and Professor W. E. Hocking for
a number of quotations from *The Meaning of God in
Human Experience* and *Human Nature and its Remaking*.

I am also indebted to the following who have allowed me to
reproduce quotations which I know only through their inclusion
in the collections named :

Great Souls at Prayer, published by H. R. Allenson.
A Book of Devotional Readings, by the Rev. J. M. Connell
(Longmans, Green & Co.).
Songs of Praise, edited by Percy Dearmer, R. Vaughan
Williams and Martin Shaw (Oxford University Press).

It has been necessary to prepare the book for the press in
the midst of preparations for a visit to Africa. If any passage
has been quoted for which permission has not been sought and
acknowledgment made I trust that the unintentional oversight
may be pardoned. If my attention is called to any such
omission, full acknowledgment will be made in any subsequent
edition.

My wife has collaborated with me in the preparation of the
Diary, has typewritten the manuscript, and checked all the
quotations. Without her help the Diary could not have been
published.

J. H. OLDHAM.

Life

In him was life; and the life was the light of men.

We have seen, and . . . declare unto you the life, the eternal life, which was with the Father, and was manifested unto us.— God gave unto us eternal life, and this life is in his Son.—The law of the Spirit of life in Christ Jesus made me free from the law of sin and of death.

The Fourth Gospel opens with the great thesis, " In him was life." It closes with the emphatic statement of its main purpose, " that believing, ye may have life through his name." These two verses may be regarded as the poles between which the thought of the Gospel revolves. The eternal need of man is for life, more abundant life. It is the one comprehensive word which sums up all the thousand wants and longings of our human nature.

The spirit of man craves not comfort, but liberty, not economic stability or equitable administration, but the right, at the cost of infinite toil and tribulation, to work out its own salvation. Its desire in all ages is not for happiness, but for life.

Jesus' teaching is a teaching of life. Life cannot be taught, it can only be lived and known. Those alone understand the teaching of Jesus who know that it is not teaching at all, but simply the living utterance of one who had achieved rebirth into a new condition of life. Its purpose is to create this new life in others, and in those who have ears to hear it new life is immediately born.

The strength of Christianity consists in its being primarily not a view, but a life, a spiritual, religious life, requiring, implying, definite doctrines concerning God and man, and their relations to each other, but never exhausted by these doctrines even in their collectivity, inexhaustible though these in their turn are by their union with the life of the spirit, their origin and end.

What makes a man a Christian is neither his intellectual acceptance of certain ideas nor his conformity to a certain rule, but his possession of a certain Spirit and his participation in a certain Life.

Almighty God, who through thy Son Jesus Christ hast opened unto us the gate of everlasting life, grant that with open hearts we may receive thy gift of life and be renewed in mind and body; and that thy power may work in us to do thy will.

More Abundant Life

I came that they may have life, and may have it abundantly.

As dying, and behold, we live.—In everything commending ourselves, as ministers of God, in much patience, in necessities, in distresses . . . in pureness, in knowledge, in longsuffering, in kindness, in the Holy Ghost, in love unfeigned.—In all these things we are more than conquerors.

No, my brothers, I deem not, I, that I have grasped it yet; but one thing I *can* say—this, that I forget all the course left behind, that I strain on, on, over that which stretches before me : with the goal in view am I racing on, onward to the prize to which God is calling us upward, the life in Messiah Jesus.

To live is to meet life eager and unafraid, to refuse none of its challenges, to evade none of its responsibilities, to go forth daily with a gay and adventurous heart to encounter its risks, to overcome its difficulties and to seize its opportunities with both hands.

> Life is—to wake, not sleep,
>   Rise and not rest, but press
> From earth's level where blindly creep
>   Things perfected, more or less,
> To the heaven's height, far and steep.
>
> The fighter's strength, the echoing strife,
> The high tumultuous lists of life.
>
> Was there naught better than to enjoy ?
>   No feat which, done, would make time break,
>   And let us pent-up creatures through
>   Into eternity, our due ?
> No forcing earth to teach heaven's employ ?

Christianity is essentially, centrally, a heroism.

Grant to us, O Lord, the royalty of inward happiness and the serenity which comes from living close to thee. Daily renew in us the sense of Joy, and let the eternal Spirit of the Father dwell in our souls and bodies, filling every corner of our hearts with light and courage, so that, bearing about with us the infection of a good courage, we may be diffusers of life, and may meet all ills and cross accidents with gallant and high-hearted happiness, giving thee thanks always for all things.

God's Beloved Son

And a voice came out of the heavens, Thou art my beloved Son, in thee I am well pleased.

No one knoweth . . . the Father, save the Son, and he to whomsoever the Son willeth to reveal him.—When the fulness of the time came, God sent forth his Son.—The Son can do nothing of himself, but what he seeth the Father doing : for what things soever he doeth, these the Son also doeth in like manner.

Jesus knew that he and the God whom he sought were one. Yet more than one, two in an ineffable relation of unity, so complete and so peaceful, so far beyond all that the intellect could comprehend of union between two, that there was but one human relation that would not wholly betray the truth. Father and Son.

In the Gospel of the Hebrews there is a different version of the voice which Jesus heard. It reads : " My son, in all the prophets did I await thee, that thou mightest come and I might rest in thee, for thou art my rest." God had longed for his son, for one who should know his secret heart. Now one had not faltered : his son was born. Jesus believed himself to be the son of God. Such a belief is scarcely imaginable by our minds. If we desire to conceive it—and we must make the effort, in order to understand him—we must take these two things into our reckoning : that he built his whole life upon this belief, and that his life changed the history of the world. After Jesus lived and died in it, the world was never the same again. A new and spiritual energy entered into the process of human life. It is not exhausted; so far as one can see it never will be exhausted; and it may only now be entering upon a phase of plenary power.

> O feet so strong to climb the path of duty,
>   O lips divine that taught the words of truth,
> Kind eyes that marked the lilies in their beauty,
>   And heart that kindled at the zeal of youth.

O God, our Shepherd, give to the Church a new vision and a new charity, new wisdom and fresh understanding; that the eternal message of thy Son, undefiled by the traditions of men, may be hailed as the good news of the new age; through him who maketh all things new, Jesus Christ our Lord.

First-born Among Many Brethren

Foreordained to be conformed to the image of his Son, that he might be the first-born among many brethren.

When the fulness of the time came, God sent forth his Son . . . that we might receive the adoption of sons.—The earnest expectation of the creation waiteth for the revealing of the sons of God . . . in hope that the creation itself also shall be delivered from the bondage of corruption into the liberty of the glory of the children of God.—Behold what manner of love the Father hath bestowed upon us, that we should be called children of God. . . . Now are we children of God, and it is not yet made manifest what we shall be. We know that if he shall be manifested, we shall be like him. . . . Every one that hath this hope set on him purifieth himself, even as he is pure.

His wonderful news was simply this : that all men were God's sons, if they would but become his sons. This was, and is, and ever will be, the wonderful news of Jesus. Men have seldom believed in it, though they have believed in things concerning him far more incredible than this. Men were to become sons of God ; if they would become sons of God, they and all things would be changed. Not gently changed in the sense that bad men would become good, but radically, catastrophically changed. A new kind of life, a new order of consciousness would begin, as different from that which men now have as human life and human consciousness is different from animal life and animal consciousness. Between these there is an abyss. Such an abyss mankind would have leaped when they became sons of God.

In the Greek world, along with the free-man's privilege of speech, went the free-man's responsibility to take counsel for, and fight the battles of, the state. So it is in Christ's teaching. If God's sons are free, they must enter into his purposes and fight his battles.

> Servants of God !—or sons
> Shall I not call you ? because
> Not as servants ye knew
> Your Father's innermost mind,
> His, who unwillingly sees
> One of his little ones lost—
> Yours is the praise if mankind
> Hath not as yet in its march
> Fainted, and fallen, and died !

O God, the Father of mercies, grant unto us ever to hold fast to the spirit of adoption, whereby we cry to thee "Father," and are called, and are, thy sons.

A Man

A man shall be as an hiding place from the wind, and a covert from the tempest; as rivers of water in a dry place, as the shadow of a great rock in a weary land.

As God has chosen to reveal his inmost nature in the beauty of a human life and to bring redemption and salvation to the world through the filial response and heroic achievement of one who lived on earth as his Son, so it is always through the faith, steadfastness and sacrifice of some individual that the sores of the world are healed, wrongs righted, and peace and happiness, truth and justice established among men.

> Then, in such hour of need
> Of your fainting, dispirited race,
> Ye, like angels, appear,
> Radiant with ardour divine !
> Beacons of hope, ye appear !
> Languor is not in your heart,
> Weakness is not in your word,
> Weariness not on your brow,
> Ye alight in our van ! at your voice,
> Panic, despair, flee away.
> Ye move through the ranks, recall
> The stragglers, refresh the outworn,
> Praise, re-inspire the brave !
> Order, courage, return.

Thou hast thy way to go, thou hast thy day
To live ; thou hast thy need of thee to make
In the heart of others ; do thy thing ; yea, slake
The world's great thirst for yet another man !

O how comely it is and how reviving
To the spirits of just men long oppressed !
When God into the hands of their deliverer
Puts invincible might
To quell the mighty of the earth, th' oppressor,
The brute and boisterous force of violent men. . . .
He all their ammunition
And feat of war defeats
With plain heroic magnitude of mind
And celestial vigour armed.

Hold us this day, O God, in thy keeping, and grant to us thy spirit of beauty and truth, that around us, wherever we go, loveliness, purity, joy, may leap into splendid being.

The Principle of Alternation

Jesus went out into the mountain to pray; and he continued all night in prayer to God.

My meat is to do the will of him that sent me, and to accomplish his work.—The Son of man came eating and drinking.

God and the world must be worked in with one another for ever : for ever they must be pursued in alternation.

As the body can live only by inhalation and exhalation; and as the mind can only flourish by looking out for sensible material and then elaborating and spiritualizing it : so the soul can live, to be fully normal in normal circumstances, only by a double process : occupation with the concrete and then abstraction from it, and this alternately, on and on.

Our powers become rapidly exhausted in our work. If we occupy ourselves exclusively with the world, even for the purpose of serving it, we become worldly, superficial, unreal and ineffective.

> Still-born silence, thou that art
> Floodgate of the deeper heart.

We cannot live well unless there is something in our lives which offers us from time to time the possibility of absolute detachment and solitude.

When we have caught the spirit of this kind of detachment we discover that the outer dimension of ourself varies with the greatness of the thing we are over against quite as truly as with the greatness of the thing allied to us.

I cannot praise a fugitive and cloistered virtue, unexercised and unbreathed, that never sallies out and sees her adversary, but slinks out of the race, where that immortal garland is to be run for, not without dust and heat.

Our Father, who art in heaven, grant that as thy Son, Jesus Christ, held secret communion with thee, and came forth from that communion into the world of men to manifest in the common incidents and in the testing experiences of life thy divine glory, so there may be in us the same rhythm of a life that is both raised above the world and lived fearlessly and unshrinkingly in the world.

Christ Liveth in Me

I live; and yet no longer I, but Christ liveth in me.

It is only in the adoption of a creative attitude towards our environment, in the endeavour to save others, that the instincts, and the will which is formed out of them, can find their complete and ultimate satisfaction. We ourselves, that is to say, can be saved or remade only by trying to save and remake our fellows. But here arises a dilemma. How can we save others when we are not yet saved ourselves? Is there not in the endeavour an element of unpardonable presumption? Christianity proposes a way out. It relieves us at once of the burden of supposing that it is through any merit or power of our own that we can save others. It is nothing inherent in us that is to do the work, but something in which we *participate*.

Thus with every element of self-assertion in the work of saving human nature comes in the same instant its antidote: "Yet not I, but whatever I have found visibly divine in the world, worketh in me." There is power in the world, and such power as I must wield if I am to find what I mean by living; but that power, even if it resides in me for a moment, is very little mine. Far from a testimony to my ability if I accomplish something with it, it is a comment on my culpable lack of faith if I fail to work miracles with it.

One of the greatest discoveries a man can make is to awake to the fact that the power with which he has to do his work is not his power at all, and that consequently his own sufficiency, his past experience and his present feelings may be disregarded and his whole reliance placed on the unchanging forces of truth, goodness and love which he may allow to work in and through him. The scale by which the possibilities of his achievement are measured is thus entirely changed.

> O live in us this day.
> O clothe thyself, thy purpose yet again
> In human clay:
> Work through our feebleness thy strength,
> Work through our meanness thy nobility,
> Work through our helpless poverty of soul
> Thy grace, thy glory and thy love.

To-Day

To-day, oh that ye would hear his voice !

Another day had dawned, wherein God bids us live eternal life,
Shake loose the bonds of time and death,
Step clear together from the iron chains of fate
Into his own dominion, his own perfect home
Of freedom, light and joy.

All occasions invite his mercies, and all times are his seasons.

> Look to this Day,
> For it is Life, the very Life of Life ;
> In its brief course lie all the varieties of Existence,
> The Bliss of Growth,
> The Glory of Action,
> The Splendour of Beauty. . . .
> Look well therefore to this day.

Say to thy Soul : "Soul, wait awhile ! Enter not so heedlessly upon the daily round. Bethink thee, this is a day which
it hath cost God long ages to fashion forth. For it had to grow
out of yesterday—out of thy doings, and others' doings, and
his own thought and help and patience, throughout the hours
that now are yesterday and all through the days that went to
make of yesterday what yesterday was. Wherefore this day,
which seemeth to thee so like unto other days that thy acquired
capacities and experiences might suffice for competent discharge of its affairs, is indeed not like but different. It is
God's newest handiwork, the fruit of his longest patience.
Darest thou lay on it thy clumsy fingers, until first, in the quiet,
his commission shall have sounded in thine ears afresh, and
he shall have passed his promise to inspire thy weak
endeavour ? "

> At thy feet, O Christ, we lay
> Thine own gift of this new day ;
> Doubt of what it holds in store
> Makes us crave thine aid the more ;
> Lest it prove a time of loss,
> Mark it, Saviour, with thy Cross.

Grant us, O Lord, to pass this day in gladness and peace,
without stumbling and without stain ; that, reaching the even-
tide victorious over all temptation, we may praise thee, the
eternal God, who dost govern all things.

The Babe in the Manger

And she brought forth her firstborn son; and she wrapped him
in swaddling clothes, and laid him in a manger, because there
was no room for them in the inn.

> They all were looking for a king
> To slay their foes and lift them high;
> Thou cam'st, a little baby thing,
>   That made a woman cry.

> Mother of God ! no lady thou :
>   Common wóman of common earth,
> *Our Lady* ladies call thee now;
>   But Christ was never of gentle birth :
>   A common man of common earth. . . .
> And still for men to come she sings,
>   Nor shall her singing pass away.
> " *He hath filled the hungry with good things* "—
>   Oh, listen, lords and ladies gay,
> " *And the rich he hath sent empty away.*"

> There fared a mother driven forth
>   Out of an inn to roam;
> In the place where she was homeless
>   All men are at home.
> The crazy stable close at hand,
> With shaking timber and shifting sand,
> Grew a stronger thing to abide and stand
>   Than the square stones of Rome. . . .
> Here we have battle and blazing eyes,
> And chance and honour and high surprise;
> But our homes are under miraculous skies
>   Where the Yule tale was begun.

> Though Christ a thousand times
>   In Bethlehem be born,
> If he's not born in thee,
>   Thy soul's forlorn.

O Father, who hast declared thy love to men by the birth
of the Holy Child at Bethlehem; help us to welcome him with
gladness and to make room for him in our common days; so
that we may live at peace with one another and in good-will
with all thy family; through the same thy Son, Jesus Christ
our Lord

The Angel's Song

And suddenly there was with the angel a multitude of the heavenly host praising God, and saying, Glory to God in the highest, and on earth peace among men in whom he is well pleased.

> For if such holy song
> Inwrap our fancy long,
>   Time will run back and fetch the age of gold,
> And speckled Vanity
> Will sicken soon and die
>   And leprous Sin will melt from earthly mould;
> And Hell itself will pass away,
> And leave her dolorous mansions to the peering day.
>
> Yea, Truth and Justice then
> Will down return to men,
>   Orb'd in a rainbow; and, like glories wearing,
> Mercy will sit between,
> Throned in celestial sheen,
>   With radiant feet the tissued clouds down steering :
> And heaven, as at some festival,
> Will open wide the gates of her high palace hall.

Could the world unite in the practice of that despised train of virtues, which the divine ethics of our Saviour hath so inculcated upon us, the furious face of things must disappear; Eden would be yet to be found, and the angels might look down, not with pity, but with joy upon us.

> Visions of glory, spare my aching sight :
> Ye unborn ages, crowd not on my soul.

Life can have little meaning for us without the faith that the things which we know in our hearts to be highest will one day be triumphant.

O Thou who givest visions unto them that praise thee, give us also the courage to make our dreams come true. Help us to know that the ideal cannot evade us for ever; that it is knocking at the door, and is an urgent pressure upon life, hungering to become actual, to the praise of Jesus Christ our Lord.

Man's True Life

Man shall not live by bread alone, but by every word that proceedeth out of the mouth of God.

God said, Let us make man in our image, after our likeness. —As for man, his days are as grass; but the mercy of the Lord is from everlasting to everlasting . . . and his righteousness unto children's children.—I can do all things in him that strengtheneth me.—The things which are impossible with men are possible with God.

> Sure, he that made us with such large discourse,
> Looking before and after, gave us not
> That capability and godlike reason
> To fust in us unused.

> To suffer woes which Hope thinks infinite;
> To forgive wrongs darker than death or night;
>   To defy Power, which seems omnipotent;
> To love, and bear; to hope till Hope creates
> From its own wreck the thing it contemplates;
>   Neither to change, nor falter, nor repent;
> This, like thy glory, Titan, is to be
> Good, great and joyous, beautiful and free,
> This is alone Life, Joy, Empire and Victory.

> Man, her last work, who seem'd so fair,
>   Such splendid purpose in his eyes. . . .
> Who loved, who suffer'd countless ills,
>   Who battled for the True, the Just.

While we, the brave, the mighty, and the wise,
We men, who in our morn of youth defied
The elements, must vanish;—be it so !
Enough, if something from our hands have power
To live, and act, and serve the future hour;
And if, as toward the silent tomb we go,
Through love, through hope, and faith's transcendent dower,
We feel that we are greater than we know.

> But felt through all this fleshly dress
> Bright shoots of everlastingness.

O God, who hast created man after thine own image and made him capable of discerning and striving after truth and goodness, honour and loyalty, unselfishness and purity; grant that by the power of thy indwelling Spirit we may learn to prize these above rubies and fine gold, knowing that in them we truly live.

B

God Alone to be Worshipped

Thou shalt worship the Lord thy God, and him only shalt thou serve.

My soul thirsteth for God, for the living God.—My soul thirsteth for thee, my flesh longeth for thee, in a dry and weary land, where no water is.—My flesh and my heart faileth : but God is the strength of my heart and my portion for ever.

Morality for Jesus springs out of a new relation to God. It was his aim to inspire his followers with his own absolute trust in the heavenly Father, who is altogether just and good. As children of God they were to subordinate their wills to his. Their action as moral beings was to be nothing else than the outcome of this obedience. . . . In Judaism religion and right action are no doubt brought very close together. God is the upholder of righteousness, and only the righteous may stand in his presence. But Hebrew thought never attains to the idea that trust in God is itself the active principle of all goodness.

In proportion to the depth and the breadth of any and every creature's nature, the creature possesses, or can attain to, the consciousness that God is its sole ultimate rest, sole pure delight. The religious soul, in proportion to the strength of its religion, always reaches beyond all abstract law, all mere sense of duty and of obligation. Our prayer will be immensely enriched by a persistent cultivation of this sense of God as our true home. For thus the rivalry between God and creatures for the possession of our hearts will become less and less a struggle between a mysterious obligation and a clear fascination, and more and more a competition between an ocean-wide, all penetrating joy, when our souls come to their true, deep selves, and pleasures feverish, fleeting and shallow, when we allow ourselves heedlessly to be carried along by our superficial selves.

Eternal God, the light of the minds that know thee, the joy of the hearts that love thee, and the strength of the wills that serve thee ; grant us so to know thee that we may truly love thee, so to love that we may fully serve thee, to the honour and glory of thy holy Name.

Power

And Jesus returned in the power of the Spirit into Galilee.

With authority and power he commandeth the unclean spirits, and they come out.—No one can enter into the house of the strong man, and spoil his goods, except he first bind the strong man.—Ye shall receive power, when the Holy Ghost is come upon you.—The kingdom of God is not in word, but in power.—I am not ashamed of the gospel : for it is the power of God unto salvation.—Striving according to his working, which worketh in me mightily.

Force, efficiency in execution, or overt action, is one necessary constituent of character. Any other character is wishy-washy; it is goody, not good. The individual must have the power to stand up and count for something in the actual conflicts of life. He must have initiative, insistence, persistence, courage and industry. He must, in a word, have all that goes under the name " force of character."

The indispensable basis for the full development of character is an inner capacity for wide and rich experience; without this nothing great and noble can come to birth. But equally essential for the realization of the highest values is a quality of soul, the importance of which is not always sufficiently recognized, namely, an energy which can force a way through to a new level of achievement. This alone makes the acknowledgment and realization of the higher value actual. This release of new vital energy is known in the language of religion as the awakening or new birth of the soul, or as the mastery and overcoming of self.

It is our business . . . rather to run the risk of falling into faults in a course which leads us to act with effect and energy than to loiter out our days without blame and without use. Public life is a situation of power and energy; he trespasses against his duty who sleeps upon his watch, as well as he that goes over to the enemy.

Almighty God, who through thine only-begotten Son Jesus Christ hast overcome death, and opened unto us the gate of everlasting life; we humbly beseech thee, that, as by thy special grace preventing us thou dost put into our minds good desires, so by thy continual help we may bring the same to good effect; through Jesus Christ our Lord.

The Divine Call

And straightway he called them : and they left their father Zebedee in the boat with the hired servants, and went after him.

He went forth, and beheld a publican, named Levi, sitting at the place of toll, and said unto him, Follow me. And he forsook all, and rose up and followed him.—By faith Abraham, when he was called, obeyed.

A man's career and the total worth of the work of his life are determined far less by the plans which he consciously makes than by his almost unheeded response to the apparently trivial experiences of daily life. On an ordinary day, in the most familiar circumstances, at a wholly unexpected moment, he may find himself face to face with one of the real turning-points of his life. Happy is he if in that hour the voice which calls him to higher destinies and to his appointed task does not fall on deaf or unheeding ears.

> I said : " Let me walk in the fields."
> He said : " No, walk in the town."
> I said : " There are no flowers there."
> He said : " No flowers, but a crown." . . .
>
> I said : " But the air is thick,
> And fogs are veiling the sun."
> He answered : " Yet souls are sick,
> And souls in the dark undone." . . .
>
> I cast one look at the fields,
> Then set my face to the town;
> He said : " My child, do you yield?
> Will you leave the flowers for the crown ? "
>
> Then into his hand went mine;
> And into my heart came he;
> And I walk in a light divine
> The path I had feared to see.

Almighty God, who didst give such grace unto thy holy apostle Saint Andrew, that he readily obeyed the calling of thy Son Jesus Christ, and followed him without delay; grant unto us all, that we, being called by thy holy work, may forthwith give up ourselves obediently to fulfil thy holy commandments, through the same Jesus Christ, our Lord.

Prayer

And in the morning, a great while before day, he rose up and went out, and departed into a desert place, and there prayed.

It came to pass, as he was praying in a certain place, that when he ceased, one of his disciples said unto him, Lord, teach us to pray.—As he was praying, the fashion of his countenance was altered.—But thou, when thou prayest, enter into thine inner chamber, and having shut thy door, pray to thy Father which is in secret.

There cannot be the faintest doubt that prayer is the heart and centre of all religion. Religion and prayer are not identical, but are related to one another as life and breathing, as thought and speech. Just as there can be no true religion without the idea of God and of the eternal, so there can be no genuine religious life without the life of prayer.

> Prayer is the Christian's vital breath,
> The Christian's native air.

Religion, by lifting ministry up into worship, opens up infinite horizons and inexhaustible depths.

To pray is to anchor the finite will in the will of God.

> Lord, what a change within us one short hour
> Spent in thy presence will avail to make !
> What heavy burdens from our bosoms take !
> What parchèd grounds refresh as with a shower !
> We kneel, and all around us seems to lower;
> We rise, and all, the distant and the near,
> Stands forth in sunny outline, brave and clear;
> We kneel, how weak ! we rise, how full of power !
> Why, therefore, should we do ourselves this wrong,
> Or others—that we are not always strong—
> That we are sometimes overborne with care—
> That we should ever weak or heartless be,
> Anxious or troubled—when with us is prayer,
> And joy and strength and courage are with thee.

O God, who callest us to pray to thee, pardon, we beseech thee, the imperfections of all our devotions. Grant that we may be delivered from wandering thoughts, and enabled so earnestly to contemplate thy presence, that our worship of thee on earth may be a foretaste of the perfect fruition of thy Godhead in thine everlasting kingdom.

Freedom from Attachment

Blessed are the poor in spirit : for theirs is the kingdom of heaven.

Jesus looking upon him loved him, and said unto him, One thing thou lackest : go, sell whatsoever thou hast, and give to the poor, and thou shalt have treasure in heaven : and come, follow me.—Jesus saith unto him, The foxes have holes, and the birds of the heaven have nests; but the Son of man hath not where to lay his head.

Jesus again and again demanded the complete abandonment of all possessions : not because of any evil inherent in money as such, but because wealth was a mighty obstacle in the way of union with God. He believed that the possession of wealth almost inevitably involved attachment to it, and consequently an inability to receive and respond to the teaching of the kingdom. But wealth is but one form of attachment to the unregenerate life. Jesus no less peremptorily enjoined the dissolution of far more precious attachments, the abandonment of home and family. He evidently believed that a complete severance from all attachments whatsoever was a necessary preliminary of complete rebirth. But this ruthless rejection of all attachments is simply a means to the great end. The goal once attained the element of self-constraint immediately disappears. A new, rich spontaneity of life is achieved. The member of the kingdom is an absolutely free man because he is absolutely obedient to God's will.

We glorify the soldier as the man absolutely unencumbered. Owning nothing but his bare life, and willing to toss that up at any moment when the cause commands him, he is the representative of unhampered freedom in ideal directions.

" They lost all they had." Their faith ? Their godliness ? The possessions of the hidden man of the heart which in the sight of God are of great price ? Did they lose these ? For these are the wealth of Christians. But as to those feebler spirits who, though they cannot be said to prefer earthly possessions to Christ, do yet cleave to them with a somewhat immoderate attachment, they have discovered by the pain of losing these things how much they were sinning in loving them.

O God, deliver us from earthly desires, that no sin may reign in us, but that we may with free spirits serve thee, our only Lord.

The Comfort of God

Blessed are they that mourn : for they shall be comforted.

I, even I, am he that comforteth you.—He that comforteth the lowly, even God.—Blessed be the God and Father of our Lord Jesus Christ, the Father of mercies and God of all comfort; who comforteth us in all our affliction, that we may be able to comfort them that are in any affliction through the comfort wherewith we ourselves are comforted of God.

> Woe ! woe ! to those who placidly suspire,
> Drowned in security, remote from fire ;
> Who under the dim sky and whispering trees
> By peaceful slopes and passing streams have ease. . . .
> No sacred pang disturbs their secular life.
> Eluding splendour and escaping strife ;
> They die not, for they lived not. . . .
> To those whom he doth love God hath not sent
> Such dread security, such sad content. . . .
> But he hath branded on such souls his name,
> And he will know them by the scars of flame. . . .
> So fear not grief, fear not the anguish, thou,
> The paining heart, the clasped and prostrate brow ;
> This is the emblem, and this is the sign
> By which God singles thee for fields divine.

> Joy and woe are woven fine,
> A clothing for the soul divine :
> Under every grief and pine
> Runs a joy with silken twine.

Without the experience of suffering a man's nature remains shallow. Pain that has been lived through gives to character a depth that seldom comes from the experience of happiness.

> Some source of consolation from above,
> Secret refreshings, that repair his strength,
> And fainting spirits uphold.

Comfort, we beseech thee, most gracious God, thy servants who are cast down and faint of heart amidst the sickness and sorrow of the world; and grant that by the power of thy Holy Spirit they may be enabled to go upon their way rejoicing.

Meekness

Blessed are the meek : for they shall inherit the earth.

Behold, thy King cometh unto thee, meek.—Learn of me; for I am meek and lowly in heart.—I intreat you by the meekness and gentleness of Christ.—Shewing all meekness toward all men.—The incorruptible apparel of a meek and quiet spirit, which is in the sight of God of great price.—The meek will he guide in judgment : and the meek will he teach his way.

> And there the lion's ruddy eyes
> Shall flow with tears of gold,
> And pitying the tender cries,
> And walking round the fold,
> Saying : Wrath by his meekness,
> And, by his health, sickness
> Is driven away
> From our immortal day.

A humble, creaturely attitude towards God, the consciousness of incompleteness, of one's life being unlivable without its being lived co-operatively between the soul and God, is the fundamentally and characteristically Christian attitude and moral disposition. So long as one is able by daily practice and prayer to regain this spirit one has the germ of full life, and is still living, in one's degree, the one true life and moving in the one true direction. It is just the love of this childlike, creaturely spirit, which is the *fine fleur* of Christianity, and an utterly supernatural, costing spirit and life.

In ceasing to contend for his own rights against others a man makes the rights of all others his own. Meekness is the complete absence of self-assertion in one for whom the common welfare of men has become identified with his own.

> And of his port as meke as is a mayde.
> He never yet no vileinye ne sayde
> In al his lyf unto no maner wight.
> He was a verray parfit, gentle knight.

O Almighty God, give to thy servant a meek and gentle spirit, that I may be slow to anger and easy to mercy and forgiveness. Let me ever be courteous and easy to be entreated. Let no sickness or cross accident, no employment or weariness, make me angry or ungentle or discontented or unthankful, or uneasy to them that minister to me; but in all things make me like unto the holy Jesus.

Desire

Blessed are they that hunger and thirst after righteousness :
for they shall be filled.

My soul thirsteth for thee, my flesh longeth for thee, in a
dry and weary land, where no water is.—My heart and my
flesh cry out unto the living God.—He satisfieth the longing
soul, and the hungry soul he filleth with good.—He will fulfil
the desire of them that fear him; he also will hear their cry,
and will save them.

God has called us to a share in his creative power, and our
desire is an element in the creation of the world of to-morrow.

When the soul shares the purpose of God, not coldly, but
with eager desire, then there is a new fact in the spiritual world.
A new way is opened whereby the Lord can enter into the
hearts of men.

> Above the smoke and stir of this dim spot,
> Which men call Earth, and with low-thoughted care,
> Confined, and pestered in this pinfold here,
> Strive to keep up a frail and feverish being,
> Unmindful of the crown that virtue gives. . . .
> Yet some there be that by due steps aspire
> To lay their just hands on that golden key
> That opes the palace of eternity.

> But prudence, prudence is the deadly sin,
> And one that groweth deep into a life,
> With hardening roots that clutch about the breast.
> For this refuses faith in the unknown powers
> Within man's nature; shrewdly bringeth all
> Their inspiration of strange eagerness
> To a judgment bought by safe experience;
> Narrows desire into the scope of thought.
> But it is written in the heart of man,
> Thou shalt no larger be than thy desire.

Yes, and his Spirit too—for his compassion matches our
yearning—is ever taking our human frailty by the hand. *We*
are not even sure what boons should rightly be the objects of
our prayers; but his Spirit—his very Spirit—is pleading ever
for us with sighings such as no language can shape into words.

Almighty and everlasting God, give unto us the increase of
faith, hope, and charity; and, that we may obtain that which
thou dost promise, make us to love that which thou dost
command.

Mercy

Blessed are the merciful : for they shall obtain mercy.

Shouldest not thou also have had mercy on thy fellow-servant, even as I had mercy on thee ?—Be ye merciful, even as your Father is merciful.—Go ye and learn what this meaneth, I desire mercy, and not sacrifice.

The emphasis in Jesus' teaching is all thrown on the duty of kindness which we owe to others, and little is said of justice. This has always been felt to be one of the chief difficulties in the Christian ethic. In all times the law of Christian kindness has been hard to reconcile with that of ordinary justice. Jesus' attitude is doubtless to be explained in large measure from his profound sense that justice is the prerogative of God. We must leave justice to God, who knows all things, and be content with the exercise of kindness which is in our power. There can be no question that in the final issue this position of Jesus is unanswerable. Indiscriminate kindness may be blamed for many evils, but infinitely more harm has been wrought by man's blundering efforts to do justice.

> The quality of mercy is not strained,
> It droppeth as the gentle rain from heaven
> Upon the place beneath : it is twice blest ;
> It blesseth him that gives, and him that takes.
> Though justice be thy plea, consider this,
> That, in the course of justice, none of us
> Should see salvation : we do pray for mercy ;
> And that same prayer doth teach us all to render
> The deeds of mercy.

He (John Howard) has visited all Europe—not to survey the sumptuousness of palaces, or the stateliness of temples ; not to make accurate measurements of the remains of ancient grandeur, nor to form a scale of the curiosity of modern art ; not to collect medals, or collate manuscripts : but to dive into the depths of dungeons ; to plunge into the infection of hospitals ; to survey the mansions of sorrow and pain ; to take the gauge and dimensions of misery, depression and contempt ; to remember the forgotten, to attend to the neglected, to visit the forsaken, and to compare and to collate the distresses of all men in all countries.

O holy and ever-blessed Lord, teach us to be merciful even as thou art merciful : that so we may continually follow after thee in all our doings, and be more and more conformed to thine image and likeness.

The Pure in Heart

Blessed are the pure in heart : for they shall see God.

Who shall ascend into the hill of the Lord ?   And who shall
stand in his holy place ?   He that hath clean hands, and a
pure heart.—The end of the charge is love out of a pure heart
and a good conscience and faith unfeigned.—Pure religion and
undefiled before our God and Father is this . . . to keep himself
unspotted from the world.

> This sanctuary of my soul
> Unwitting I keep white and whole
> Unlatched and lit, if thou should'st care
> To enter or to tarry there.

True purity, I thought, was something far more than the
narrow meaning often given to it.   It meant keeping oneself,
as the Bible says, altogether unspotted from the world, free
from all tyranny and stain, whether of flesh or spirit, defying
the universe to touch even the outworks of the sanctuary
which is one's soul.   It must be defiant, not the inert, fragile
crystal, but the supple, shining sword.

Purity—that immensely virile virtue.

> So dear to heaven is saintly chastity,
> That when a soul is found sincerely so,
> A thousand liveried angels lackey her,
> Driving far off each thing of sin and guilt,
> And in clear dream and solemn vision
> Tell her of things that no gross ear can hear,
> Till oft converse with heavenly habitants
> Begin to cast a beam on th' outward shape.

It is one of the most remarkable features of Christ's moral
teaching that he does not command us to regulate or control
our unlawful desires, but pronounces it unlawful to have such
desires at all.

> Still to the lowly soul
>   He doth himself impart,
> And for his dwelling and his throne
>   Chooseth the pure in heart.

O God, deliver us from earthly desires, that no sin may
reign in us, but that we may with free spirits serve thee, our
only Lord; through Jesus Christ.

Peacemakers

Blessed are the peacemakers : for they shall be called sons of God.

On earth peace, among men in whom he is well pleased.— I came not to send peace, but a sword.—The God of peace be with you all.—Having shod your feet with the preparation of the gospel of peace.

The peace of which Jesus speaks is not a negative thing. It is not dearth of trouble or the absence of pain. It is an achievement of creative minds, the triumph of the human spirit over discord, confusion and strife. From the man whose mind is at rest, whose conscience is at peace, whose will is one with the will of God, whose affections are satisfied through communion with the Eternal Joy, there emanates a beneficent and healing influence which creates a new atmosphere and raises the life of those about him to a new level of harmonious co-operation.

So have they sought to make men's minds too uniform and harmonical, by not breaking them sufficiently to contrary motions. . . . Men ought so to procure serenity as they destroy not magnanimity.

> Ah ! when shall all men's good
> Be each man's rule, and universal Peace
> Lie like a shaft of light across the land ?

> Earth shall be fair, and all her people one :
> Not till that hour shall God's whole will be done.

With malice toward none; with charity for all; with firmness in the right, as God gives us to see the right, let us strive on to finish the work we are in; to bind up the nation's wounds, to care for him who shall have borne the battle, and for his widow and his orphan—to do all which may achieve and cherish a just and lasting peace.

O God, who art peace everlasting, whose chosen reward is the gift of peace, and who hast taught us that the peacemakers are thy children, pour thy peace into our souls, that everything discordant may utterly vanish, and all that makes for peace be sweet to us for ever.

The Reward of Conflict

Blessed are they that have been persecuted for righteousness' sake : for theirs is the kingdom of heaven. Blessed are ye when men shall reproach you, and persecute you, and say all manner of evil against you falsely, for my sake. Rejoice, and be exceedingly glad : for great is your reward in heaven.

Only through opposition and contradiction can the reality, power and richness of the new life of the kingdom of heaven be fully known.

The most spiritual men, provided that they are at the same time the bravest, experience by far the most painful tragedies; but this is the very reason why they reverence life, because it offers them its greatest oppositions. It is the greatness of the danger that reveals the knight, or rather that creates him.

At the beginning of his new life the Servitor thought that he had been wholly and pre-eminently well-pleasing to God, but without labour and suffering. Now it happened once when he went forth into the country to preach that he entered a ship on the Lake of Constance; and there sat among the other passengers a comely youth in brave attire. Going forward to him he asked him what manner of man he was. " I am an esquire-errant," said the youth, " and I bring the gentlemen together, so that they may feast and tilt and fight and pay homage to fair ladies." . . . "Tell me," said the Servitor, "if a man were only brave in the first onset, would that be enough ? " "No," was the reply, " he must remain firm to the end of the tournament, and though the blows which he receives bring sparks of fire into his eyes and make the blood flow from his face, he must endure them all, if he is to obtain the glory of victory." . . . At these words the Servitor was greatly impressed, and sighing deeply, he exclaimed, " Ah ! glorious Lord God ! must the knights of this world endure so much suffering for so small a reward ! How fitting then it is that one should endure much greater labours for the everlasting prize."

> Fight the good fight with all thy might,
> Christ is thy strength, and Christ thy right;
> Lay hold on life, and it shall be
> Thy joy and crown eternally.

Grant us thy strength, O Lord, that we may consider him who endured such gainsaying of sinners against himself, and may endure hardness as good soldiers of Jesus Christ.

The Christian Witness

Ye are the light of the world.　A city set on a hill cannot be hid.

Even so let your light shine before men, that they may see your good works, and glorify your Father which is in heaven.— Ye are the salt of the earth : but if the salt have lost its savour, wherewith shall it be salted ?—Children of God without blemish in the midst of a crooked and perverse generation, among whom ye are seen as lights in the world, holding forth the word of life.—Giving no occasion of stumbling in anything, that our ministration be not blamed; but in everything commending ourselves, as ministers of God, in much patience, in afflictions, in necessities, in distresses . . .; in pureness, in knowledge, in longsuffering, in kindness, in the Holy Ghost, in love unfeigned, in the word of truth, in the power of God.—The fruit of the Spirit is love, joy, peace, longsuffering, kindness, goodness, faithfulness, meekness, temperance.

The aim of the Christian life is simple.　It is to reflect each day and in every relation the mind of God, and to reveal to men his goodness, his truth and his love.

When we have seen with our own eyes but one life guided by Christian values we know what is meant by the beauty and winsomeness of Christ.

Thee would man praise; man, but a particle of thy creation; man, that bears about him his mortality, the witness of his sin; yet man would praise thee; he, but a particle of thy creation.

> Be still the leaven
> That spreading in this dull and clodded earth
> Gives it a touch ethereal—a new birth.

A light cannot fail to be seen, unless it is prevented from shining.　But Christ knew that there would be strong temptation for men to hide their light.　It would draw the world's attention to them and so expose them to the ill-will of such as hate the light.　Cowards can always find plausible excuses for the policy of obscuration.

May God kindle in us, to his glory, the flame of his indwelling presence, that our lives may shine as stars.

The Divine Likeness

That ye may be sons of your Father which is in heaven.

Love your enemies, and pray for them that persecute you; that ye may be sons of your Father which is in heaven : for he maketh his sun to rise on the evil and the good, and sendeth rain on the just and the unjust.—Be ye therefore imitators of God.—The earnest expectation of the creation waiteth for the revealing of the sons of God.

Because all those scattered rays of beauty and loveliness which we behold spread up and down all the world over, are only the emanations of that unexhausted Light which is above; therefore should we love them all in that, and climb up always by those sunbeams unto the eternal Father of Lights : we should look upon him and take from him the pattern of our lives, and, always eyeing him, should polish and shape our souls into the clearest resemblance of him . . .; in all our dealing with men, doing good, showing mercy and compassion, advancing justice and righteousness, being always full of charity and good works; and look upon ourselves as having nothing to do here but to display and blazon the glory of our Heavenly Father.

What are the attributes of God, as we discern them in his treatment of men ? These and no others must be deemed the highest. To manifest them in our own lives must be our chief aim and glory. In our narrow sphere we are to act as God does in his, " that we may be children of our Father which is in heaven." In every act of justice and compassion we become for that moment one with God, and by constant obedience to his will we live the divine life. By living as God requires we become like God, and so realize in ourselves more of the divine life.

Whence St. Francis, seeing so much courtesy and good-will in him said : " Know, most dearly beloved brother, that courtesy is one of the properties of God, who gives his sun and rain to the just and the unjust by courtesy; and courtesy is the sister of charity, by which hatred is extinguished and love is cherished."

O God, whose blessed Son was manifested that he might destroy the works of the devil, and make us sons of God, and heirs of eternal life; grant us, we beseech thee, that, having this hope, we may purify ourselves, even as he is pure; that, when he shall appear again with power and great glory, we may be made like unto him in his eternal and glorious kingdom.

Non-Resistance

Resist not him that is evil: but whosoever smiteth thee on thy right cheek, turn to him the other also. And if any man would go to law with thee, and take away thy coat, let him have thy cloke also. And whosoever shall compel thee to go one mile, go with him twain.

These commands seem not alone to admit but to assert an abandonment of justice. For the commentary explains that they are one aspect of the perfection of God, who makes his sun to rise on the evil and the good. In other words, that which to some minds appears as the total moral indifference of nature is here held up as the perfection of God. To argue thus is to forget that what is mechanical behaviour in the inorganic realm is no longer mechanical in the realm of stimulus and response. In this realm to refuse to respond in kind may be the precise opposite of a mechanical attitude. Non-resistance may enter the situation with the force of a new idea. The new idea in the mind of the attacker, however, might be one of several: he might conclude that you were too dead to fight, or that you were too much alive to fight. Christianity depends on the possibility of putting significance into the latter idea. And the persistent refusal to criticize or to retaliate can be a sign of more life, rather than less, only when it is a response to a greater degree of truth. It must mean that the self which does injury is seen to be other than the real self; and non-resistance is an appeal from the actual self to the self that may be. In this case, it is not injustice, but it is justice to the living and changeable. Greek justice, distributive or retributive, took men statically, as they presented themselves. This type of justice refuses to take a man at his own estimate of himself; it insists on the self that *must be* and which this resolve of the non-resisting will will help to bring into being. It is a justice done for the first time to the plasticity and responsiveness of human nature; it is an absolute, or creative, justice.

> Who overcomes
> By force, hath overcome but half his foe.

Almighty God, whose ways are not our ways, and whose thoughts are higher than our thoughts, grant to us the light of thy Holy Spirit, so that more and more we may have the mind of Christ and become the children of our Father, which is in heaven.

An Absolute Standard

Take heed that ye do not your righteousness before men
. . . else ye have no reward with your Father which is in
heaven.

But thou, when thou prayest, enter into thine inner chamber,
and having shut thy door, pray to thy Father which is in secret,
and thy Father which seeth in secret shall recompense thee.—
But with me it is a very small thing that I should be judged
of you, or of man's judgment : . . . but he that judgeth me
is the Lord.—Be not afraid of them which kill the body, but are
not able to kill the soul : but rather fear him which is able to
destroy both soul and body in hell.—How can ye believe, which
receive glory one of another, and the glory that cometh from
the only God ye seek not?

A man is not free unless he is delivered from persistent side-
long anxiety about his immediate effectiveness, from servitude
to an incalculable, if not whimsical, human flux. He is free
only if he can mentally direct all his work to a constant and
absolute judgment, address his daily labour, if you like, to God,
build his houses to God and not to men, write his books to
God, in the State serve his God only, love his God in the family,
and fight against the devil and the devil alone. Kepler's
famous words are the words of the free man in this sense : "Here
I cast the die, and write a book to be read, whether by con-
temporaries or posterity, I care not. I can wait for readers
thousands of years, seeing that God waited six thousand years
for someone to contemplate his work."

If you can talk with crowds and keep your virtue
    Or walk with Kings—nor lose the common touch,
If neither foes nor loving friends can hurt you,
    If all men count with you, but none too much. . . .

Who, whether praise of him must walk the earth
For ever, and to noble deeds give birth,
Or he must fall, to sleep without his fame,
And leave a dead unprofitable name—
Finds comfort in himself and in his cause ;
And, while the mortal mist is gathering, draws
His breath in confidence of Heaven's applause.

Teach us to look in all our ends
On thee for judge, and not our friends ;
That we, with thee, may walk uncowed
By fear or favour of the crowd.

C

The Holy

Our Father which art in heaven, Hallowed be thy name.

And one cried unto another, and said, Holy, holy, holy, is the Lord of Hosts : the whole earth is full of his glory.

As against all rationalizing attempts to tone it down into something less startling, the most recent research shows quite decisively that the " Kingdom " is just greatness and marvel absolute, the " wholly other " " heavenly " thing, set in contrast to the world of here and now. What of the Lord of this Kingdom, the " heavenly Father " ? As its Lord he is not less, but far more " holy," mysterious than his Kingdom. Not to realize this is to turn the Gospel of Jesus into a mere idyll. Though it is necessarily the new message of the divine Fatherhood that the parables and discourses and pronouncements of Jesus complete and fill out, it is in such a way that it always remains an overwhelming and daring paradox that he who is " in heaven " is yet " our Father." This is the resolved contrast that first brings out the deep-felt harmony in true Christian experience ; and the harmony cannot be heard aright by the man whose ear does not detect always sounding in it this sublimated " seventh."

I have had for years, increasingly, a double sense : of the large, spacious range of our ethical capacities, and of the necessity and value of an ideal and indefinite exercise for them; *and* of all this not being God, not one bit, not one bit. Until a man feels this, till it pierces his soul, he has not waked up to the specifically religious consciousness. God is emphatically *not* simply our highest selves.

God is the Absolute Cause, the ultimate Reason, the sole true End and Determiner of our existence, our persistence, our nature. God is all these things for man. Man is not one of these things for God. Thus the positions between God and man are entirely uninterchangeable. Hence the most fundamental need, duty and happiness of man is not petition, nor even contrition, nor again even thanksgiving, but *adoration*.

We praise thee, we bless thee, we worship thee, we glorify thee, we give thanks to thee for thy great glory, O Lord God, heavenly King, God the Father Almighty.

Thy Will be Done

Thy will be done, as in heaven, so on earth.

Whosoever shall do the will of my Father which is in heaven, he is my brother, and sister, and mother.—My meat is to do the will of him that sent me, and to accomplish his work.—Not every one that saith unto me, Lord, Lord, shall enter into the kingdom of heaven; but he that doeth the will of my Father which is in heaven.

The attitude which the petition expresses is not one of resignation but that of soaring aspiration and joyful dedication to a high adventure.

The essence of the Christian ethos does not consist in a contemplative immersion in Being, or in a quietistic denegation of the will, but in an active dedication of the will to a Godhead overflowingly alive, which bears within itself positive ends for the world, and opens up an immense movement for this same world.

Jesus thinks of God not as the absolute Being, but as the God of love, righteousness, holiness. These moral qualities are his essential nature, and to be one with God can be nothing else than to have in ourselves the will of God. Conscious of his mercy and justice, we are to deal in a like spirit with our fellow-men, and so realize in ourselves something of the divine nature. The demand of Jesus is not for obedience to certain moral laws but for a new will. The one thing necessary was a right relation to God—a complete harmony of our will with the divine will. He called for no mere reformation, but for a fresh beginning, a radical change of mind, which would enable men to act rightly because in their inward nature they had become new men.

Since the chief end of life is to obey the will of God, perfect obedience must imply fullness of life. Only as we conform ourselves to that higher will which is the law of our being do we realize our true life. Men are God's children, and their life achieves its purpose as they grow like him in mind and will.

> And in thy mighty will to find
> The joy, the freedom of the mind.

> In his will is our peace.

O God, set our hearts free from the service of ourselves that it may be our meat and drink to do thy will.

The Divine Supply

Give us this day our daily bread.

Behold, the birds of the heaven, that they sow not, neither do they reap, nor gather into barns; and your heavenly Father feedeth them.—My God shall fulfil every need of yours according to his riches in glory in Christ Jesus.—God is able to make all grace abound unto you; that ye, having always all sufficiency in everything, may abound unto every good work.—He hath said unto me, My grace is sufficient for thee : for my power is made perfect in weakness.—The Lord is my Shepherd; I shall not want.

The obedience to God in which Jesus finds the spring of moral action is inseparable from trust in God. In order to do his will with our whole heart we need the assurance that he is over us—upholding and directing us and giving us all things good. This conception of God's providence belongs to the very substance of Jesus' religion, but it is no less essential to his ethic. He requires us to face the perplexities of life in the confidence that God is with us. He forbids us to plan for the future since it will be ordered by God, and our duty is to obey his will in the moment that is ours. It is evident that the moral life on all its sides must be profoundly affected by this attitude of trust in God.

(Brother Lawrence said) that he had been lately sent into Burgundy to buy the provision of wine for the society, which was a very unwelcome task to him, because he had no turn for business, and because he was lame, and could not go about the boat but by rolling himself over the casks. That, however, he gave himself no uneasiness about it, nor about the purchase of the wine. That he said to God, " It was his business he was about," and that he afterwards found it very well performed.

Discouragement, fretfulness, the sense of being overburdened are a contradiction of the essential nature of the Christian life. Its distinguishing mark is a joyous confidence in the readiness and power of God to supply all the needs of his children. To meet the unexpected and disconcerting demands of each day in the assured confidence and trust which Jesus inculcated is not easy. But the question is whether he is right with his calm and confident "Be not anxious," or we with our debilitating fears.

Almighty and ever-loving God, deliver us, we beseech thee, from the unbelief and fears of our faithless hearts, and so fill us with a sense of thy power and willingness to supply all our needs, that nothing may seem too great or too hard to undertake at thy call, and that we may continually rejoice in thy sufficiency.

The Divine Forgiveness

Forgive us our debts.

Jesus seeing their faith said unto the sick of the palsy, Son, be of good cheer; thy sins are forgiven.—As God also in Christ forgave you.—In whom we have . . . the forgiveness of our trespasses, according to the riches of his grace.

One who knows that he freely serves his cause knows that he could, if he chose, become a traitor. Do any of us ever actually thus betray our own chosen cause ? If so—now that the traitor has sinned against his light and has done his little best to make chaos of his own chosen ideal—can he follow Matthew Arnold's advice and think of his sin only in so far as is indispensable to the " firm resolve to get rid of it " ? How can I get rid of it ? It is done. It is past. I am, and to the end of endless time shall remain, the doer of that wilfully traitorous deed. Whatever other value I may get, that value I retain for ever. By his own deed of treason the traitor has consigned himself . . . to what one may call the hell of the irrevocable.

The God of the New Testament is not less holy than the God of the Old Testament. The interval between the creature and him is not diminished but made absolute. That God none the less admits access to himself and intimacy with himself is not a mere matter of course; it is a grace beyond our power to apprehend, a prodigious paradox. To take this paradox out of Christianity is to make it shallow and superficial beyond recognition.

The depths of religious experience are sounded when a man awakens to the truth that, while he has nothing to hope for from himself, he may dare to hope for everything from God; that the source of his confidence does not lie in himself at all, but in the unchanging love and inexhaustible mercy of God.

Forgive me my sins, O Lord, the sins of my youth and the sins of mine age, my secret and my whispering sins, my presumptuous and my crying sins. Forgive me those sins which I know, and those sins which I know not; forgive them all, O Lord, of thy great goodness.

> Just as I am, without one plea
> But that thy blood was shed for me,
> And that thou bidd'st me come to thee,
>   O Lamb of God, I come.

The Forgiving Spirit

As we also have forgiven our debtors.

Then came Peter, and said to him, Lord, how oft shall my brother sin against me, and I forgive him? Until seven times? Jesus saith unto him, I say not unto thee, Until seven times; but, Until seventy times seven.—Love your enemies, and pray for them that persecute you; that ye may be sons of your Father which is in heaven.—Be ye kind one to another, tender-hearted, forgiving each other, even as God also in Christ forgave you.

To Jesus God's forgiveness of men's sins was a quality so characteristic and outstanding in the Divine nature that he insisted that those who were called to be the sons of their Father in heaven should above all things exhibit the same quality. Jesus is aware that the one great hindrance to right action in our dealings with other men is the unwillingness to overlook injuries. We allow ourselves to be guided by their behaviour towards ourselves, and are thus restrained from the good we are disposed to do. God's judgment of us, his recognition that we have attained to the true life, will depend on our moral likeness to himself; and this is tested by our capacity to forgive.

Yes, but *this* neighbour is your enemy; or he belongs to the wrong tribe or caste or sect. Do not consider these unhappy facts as having any bearing on your love for him. For the ethical side of the doctrine of life concerns not what you *find*, but what you *create*. Now God means this man to be a member of the community which constitutes the Kingdom of Heaven; and God loves this man accordingly.

O holy and ever-blessed Lord, teach us, we beseech thee, to love one another, to exercise forbearance and forgiveness towards our enemies; to recompense no man evil for evil, but to be merciful even as thou, our Father in heaven, art merciful : that so we may continually follow after thee in all our doings and be more and more conformed to thy image and likeness.

Deliverance from Evil

Deliver us from the evil one.

God our Saviour.—The gospel of your salvation.—The Son of man came to seek and to save that which was lost.—Receiving the end of your faith, even the salvation of your souls.—Work out your own salvation with fear and trembling; for it is God which worketh in you.—Our wrestling is not against flesh and blood, but against the principalities, against the powers, against the world-rulers of this darkness, against the spiritual hosts of wickedness in the heavenly places.

The central concern of religion is salvation. Religion is the attainment, the experience of salvation. Salvation means wholeness, deliverance from all that injures or mutilates, or hinders the growth of, the personality. It means fullness of life, well-being, strength, power, blessedness, wealth, happiness, righteousness, joy, peace. It is the complete penetration of the human by the divine.

A man can be said to be saved not alone when he is reclaimed from rebellion or criminality; he is saved in so far as he is not wasted, in so far as the human material in him gets a chance at self-expression and utilization.

I would get my imagination and my reason into the habit, not simply of looking at sin as an offence against God, but of realizing and picturing it as chiefly a shirking of some effort, or loneliness, or pain, attached to a light or to a commandment as it is offered to us, or a seeking of some pleasure, relaxation or vanity attached to the contrary course.

> Thou, who dost dwell alone—
> Thou, who dost know thine own—
> Thou, to whom all are known
> From the cradle to the grave—
>   Save, oh save !
> From the world's temptations—
>   From tribulations—
> From that fierce anguish
> Wherein we languish,
>   From that torpor deep
>   Wherein we lie asleep,
>   Heavy as death, cold as the grave,
>   Save, oh ! save !

Treasure in Heaven

Lay not up for yourselves treasures upon the earth, where moth and rust doth consume, and where thieves break through and steal : but lay up for yourselves treasures in heaven . . . : for where thy treasure is, there will thy heart be also.

Jesus said unto him, If thou wouldest be perfect, go, sell that thou hast, and give to the poor, and thou shalt have treasure in heaven : and come, follow me.—If then ye were raised together with Christ, seek the things that are above, where Christ is.

> We fix our earnest gaze, not on things seen,
>   But on the things unseen;
> For things seen are but for a fleeting moment,
>   But for all eternity are the things unseen.

Jesus perceived that wealth, prosperity, worldly security have the effect of deceiving men as to their true position.   Surrounded with those visible protections they believe that no danger can touch them, yet the safety is all the while illusory. The earthly things on which they rely may vanish in a moment, and when these are gone they find themselves quite helpless.

Nothing seems plainer than this, that if true peace and content are to be found by man at all, they cannot be found in anything temporal or secular. They must spring from a conscious intimate possession of union of heart and will with a being who knows us through and through, as no man knows another, or even himself, who contains within him an inexhaustible wealth of being which excludes all risk of satiety, who is utterly eternal and abiding. and, therefore, can never change or fail.

The primary end and function, surely, of every Church deserving of the august name is the awakening of souls to, the preparing them for, the holding before them embodiments of, *the other. life,* the life beyond the grave. Very certainly the Church has also to help in the amelioration of *this life :* but always after, and in subordination to, and penetrated by, that metaphysical, ontological, other-worldly sense and life which alone completes and satisfies fully awakened man.

I behold how some things pass away that others may replace them, but thou dost never depart, O God, my Father, supremely good, Beauty of all things beautiful. Thou madest me for thyself, and my heart is restless till it repose in thee.

An Undivided Allegiance

No man can serve two masters : for either he will hate the
one, and love the other; or else he will hold to one; and despise
the other.   Ye cannot serve God and mammon.

What fellowship had righteousness with lawlessness ?
What common meeting-ground have light and darkness ?
What concord can be between Messiah and Belial ?
What partnership can be between believers and unbelievers ?
What compact between a temple of God and idols ?
For we, we are a temple of the Living God : of us God said,
" I will dwell in their midst, I will walk among them,
And I will be their God, and my people shall they be."
Therefore, " Come out from among them, and sever yourselves,"
    saith the Lord,
" And cleave not to the unclean thing;
And I will accept you, and I will be to you a Father,
And ye shall be to me as sons and daughters."

   For early didst thou leave the world, with powers
     Fresh, undiverted to the world without,
       Firm to their mark, not spent on other things. . . .
        O life unlike to ours !
   Who fluctuate idly without term or scope,
      Of whom each strives, nor knows for what he strives,
      And each half lives a hundred different lives.

  Character is the unification of the personality through the
achievement of a dominant purpose.

  Man is more of a person, has psychologically more character ;
the more he shows of singleness of aim, the less easily he swerves
from this, and the wider and more coherent it is.

  O Lord, we acknowledge thy dominion over us; our life,
our death, our soul and body, all belong to thee.   Oh, grant
that we may willingly consecrate them all to thee, and use
them in thy service.   Become Lord of our hearts and spirits;
that the whole inner man may be brought under thy rule, and
that thy life of love and righteousness may pervade all our
thoughts and energies and the very ground of our souls.   Come,
O Lord and King, enter into our hearts, and live and reign
there for ever and ever.

          Just as I am—thy love unknown
          Has broken every barrier down—
          Now to be thine, yea, thine alone,
            O Lamb of God, I come.

Freedom from Care

Be not anxious for the morrow.

Behold the birds of the heaven, that they sow not, neither do they reap, nor gather into barns; and your heavenly Father feedeth them. Are not ye of much more value than they?— Casting all your anxiety upon him, because he careth for you.— We know that to them that love God all things work together for good.

Care is represented by Christ as one of the great enemies of the soul, as a conspicuous sign of faithlessness, and even a cause of ruin to the soul.

The future is ordered by a power outside of us, and all efforts to shape it accordingly to our own wish are vain, and can only vex and disappoint us. Such anxiety does not help but distracts and weakens. Our wisdom is to concentrate on the present duty, and by doing it with all our might we shall be better prepared to meet the future, whatever it may bring. For Jesus the world with all its dangers and accidents is overruled by God. Our part is to discern the sovereign will at work and reconcile ourselves to its behests. If we do so we shall find that the things which seemed most contrary are on our side, and are offered by God as means to our welfare. It is this trust in God which makes the moral task, as Jesus conceives it, one of freedom and joy.

Over-anxiety about to-morrow meant doubt if God could be in to-morrow. To Jesus, God was already in to-morrow. He had himself tested the life that is lived from hand to mouth. He knew that God never strove to lift his children out of that day-by-day dependence. But God never disappointed man's simple confidence. To step out from behind those false and artificial walls, which men, haunted by the ghosts of Care and Fear, sought to build against the unknown to-morrow, was like shaking off the fetters of a humiliating captivity and stepping out into freedom.

O most loving Father, who willest us to give thanks for all things, to dread nothing but the loss of thee, and to cast all our care on thee who carest for us; preserve us from faithless fears and worldly anxieties, and grant that no clouds of this mortal life may hide from us the light of that love which is immortal.

The God of Nature

Consider the lilies of the field, how they grow; . . . Solomon in all his glory was not arrayed like one of these.

Are not two sparrows sold for a farthing? and not one of them shall fall on the ground without your Father.—There was a marriage in Cana of Galilee; . . . and Jesus also was bidden, and his disciples, to the marriage.

> But on the homeward road,
> A great light came upon me, and I heard
> The God's voice singing in a nestling lark;
> Felt his sweet wonder in a swaying rose;
> Received his blessing from a wayside well;
> Looked on his beauty in a lover's face. . . .

> You've seen the world—
> The beauty and the wonder and the power,
> The shapes of things, their colours, lights and shades,
> Changes, surprises,—and God made it all !—
> For what? Do you feel thankful, ay or no,
> For this fair town's face, yonder river's line,
> The mountain round it and the sky above,
> Much more the figures of man, woman, child,
> These are the frame to? What's it all about?
> To be passed over, despised? or dwelt upon,
> Wondered at?

God is the author of, and God is variously reflected in, all innocent Nature as well as in all Supernature. He is the God revealed in high heroisms, in the sincere forgiveness of our enemies and the eager acceptance of suffering, and likewise in the beauties of external nature and in the honesties and decencies of common human life; the God not only of the Alpine heights with the edelweiss and the alpenrose, but also of the Lombard plains with their cornfields and potatoes. The recognition of this brings much help in our prayers. For in prayer it brings a tension, and also a relaxation. In both these movements of the soul God can, and should be, envisaged—in the relaxation, the God of nature, the source of all that is wholesome and homely; and in the tension, the God of Supernature, the source of all that is ardent and heroic. We thus escape dullness and monotony—the subtle dangers of the spiritual life.

O God, open our eyes to see thee everywhere; may the flowers and trees and the green grass, the sea, the sky and the stars, the birds and all the creatures thou hast made, and the works and labour of man continually speak to us of thee; that we may live as thy glad children in our Father's world.

Righteousness

Seek ye first his kingdom, and his righteousness.

Except your righteousness shall exceed the righteousness of the scribes and Pharisees, ye shall in no wise enter into the kingdom of heaven.—Thou hast loved righteousness, and hated wickedness : therefore God, thy God, hath anointed thee with the oil of gladness above thy fellows.—If ye know that he is righteous, ye know that every one also that doeth righteousness is begotten of him.

"All that you can conceive of righteousness, and of forgiving love, that," said the prophets, "is true of the one Almighty God." There is a life-or-death leap of the soul of man out into that great unknown ruling world, an intuition that fills one with wonder at its boldness. To unite religion with morality is to begin a new world. It is the question whether Force or Right is the ultimate thing in the universe, and that in the end of the day is the question whether humanity will exterminate itself or climb to undreamed-of heights of nobility and joy.

> Mortals, that would follow me,
> Love Virtue ; she alone is free,
> She can teach ye how to climb
> Higher than the sphery chime :
> Or, if Virtue feeble were,
> Heaven itself would stoop to her.

> Stern Lawgiver ! yet thou dost wear
> The Godhead's most benignant grace ;
> Nor know we any thing so fair
> As is the smile upon thy face :
> Flowers laugh before thee on their beds
> And fragrance in thy footing treads ;
> Thou dost preserve the stars from wrong ;
> And the most ancient heavens, through thee, are fresh
> and strong.

O thou who dost not suffer us to be satisfied with little things, but hast set eternity in our hearts, lead us to the spring of living water where alone our thirst can be quenched. Thou, who art the true bread that comest down from heaven, feed our spirits with food of righteousness. May we desire more than all else to be righteous as thou art righteous.

Asking and Receiving

Ask, and it shall be given you; seek, and ye shall find; knock, and it shall be opened unto you : for every one that asketh receiveth; and he that seeketh findeth; and to him that knocketh it shall be opened.

All things whatsoever ye pray and ask for, believe that ye have received them, and ye shall have them.—If ye abide in me, and my words abide in you, ask whatsoever ye will, and it shall be done unto you.—Ask, and ye shall receive, that your joy may be fulfilled.

Prayer is no mere feeling of exaltation, no mere feeling of awe, no mere abasement in the presence of the Highest; on the contrary, prayer is actual intercourse with God, a living converse of the finite spirit with the infinite. Psychological study, when it penetrates to the depths, reveals with unmistakable clearness that to pray means to speak and hold converse with God as a servant does with his master, or a child with his father, or a bride with her husband.

Average prayer, when it ventures to be specific, is apt to end upon a note of uncertainty. We remember how liable we are to ask amiss; and breathing the words " If it be thy will," we cease our prayer not knowing whether we have received what we ask. Very different would appear to be the New Testament ideal of prayer. It is not a breathing out of our perplexities and desires into an irresponsive silence; it is question and answer, request and consent or, if need be, refusal. Such definiteness and confidence of petition, so far from being a crude and almost unworthy form of prayer, requires for its possibility the highest development of filial intuition.

Of all mental exercises earnest prayer is the most severe.

God's Grace is richer than prayer : God always giveth more than he is asked.

Faith is the foundation and basis of prayer : the foundation of faith is the promise of God.

O God, our refuge and strength, who art the author of all godliness, be ready, we beseech thee, to hear the devout prayers of thy Church : and grant that those things which we ask faithfully we may obtain effectually; through Jesus Christ our Lord.

Discipline

Narrow is the gate, and straitened the way, that leadeth unto life.

Strive to enter in by the narrow door.—If thy hand or thy foot causeth thee to stumble, cut it off, and cast it from thee : it is good for thee to enter into life maimed or halt, rather than having two hands or two feet to be cast into the eternal fire.—I therefore so run, as not uncertainly; so fight I, as not beating the air.—Let us also, seeing we are compassed about with so great a cloud of witnesses, lay aside every weight, and the sin which doth so easily beset us, and let us run with patience the race that is set before us, looking unto Jesus.

Jesus saith, Except ye fast to the world, ye shall in no wise find the kingdom of God.

Renunciation is necessary, if one wants to be or to become something. To be everything at once is impossible. Entirely universal natures have no centre and consequently are without power. Not only in the greatest things, but also in the ordinary conduct of daily life, a man has to learn to renounce life in order to gain life. Above all, the demand of physical impulses to find their natural satisfaction must be victoriously resisted. Without asceticism spiritual character and achievement are impossible.

> Why comes temptation but for man to meet
> And master and make crouch beneath his foot,
> And so be pedestaled in triumph ?   Pray
> " Lead us into no such temptations, Lord ! "
> Yea, but O thou whose servants are the bold,
> Lead such temptations by the head and hair,
> Reluctant dragons, up to who dares fight,
> That so he may do battle and have praise !

Combat and concentration, hardness and asceticism are an absolutely essential constituent of the Christian outlook. Where this element is not, there is not authentic Christianity, but some sentimental humanitarianism, or some other weakening inadequacy.

I wish you, then, a very rich, deep, true, straight and simple growth in the love of God, accepted and willed gently but greatly, *at the daily, hourly cost of self.*

Teach us to-day, O Master, to rule ourselves, to be stern, harsh, merciless to our bodies and minds; to discipline our lives with an iron hand, so that no sloth of ours, no craven despair, no self-indulgence, no failure of sympathy and imagination, may mar the work of thy Kingdom.

Hearing and Doing

Not every one that saith unto me, Lord, Lord, shall enter into the kingdom of heaven; but he that doeth the will of my Father which is in heaven.

Every one therefore which heareth these words of mine, and doeth them, shall be likened unto a wise man, which built his house upon the rock : and the rain descended, and the floods came, and the winds blew, and beat upon that house; and it fell not: for it was founded upon the rock.—A man had two sons; and he came to the first, and said, Son, go work to-day in the vineyard. And he answered and said, I will not: but afterwards he repented himself, and went. And he came to the second, and said likewise. And he answered and said, I go, sir : and went not. Whether of the twain did the will of his father ?—If ye know these things, blessed are ye if ye do them.

It is not in their moment of forming, but in their moment of producing motor effects, that resolves and aspirations communicate the new " set " to the brain. . . . Seize the very first possible opportunity to act on every resolution you make, and on any emotional prompting you may experience in the direction of the habit you aspire to gain. When a resolve or a fine glow of feeling is allowed to evaporate without bearing practical fruit, it is worse than a chance lost; it works so as positively to hinder future resolutions and emotions from taking the normal path of discharge.

The only schooling to fit us for further opportunity is found in instant and unintermitting performance of present duty. No paralysis is more dangerous and fatal than procrastination. The promise of the future often lies concealed in the promptings of the moment. It is to those who hold themselves erect, on the alert, that light first rises in the darkness.

> We know the paths wherein our feet should press,
> Across our hearts are written thy decrees;
> Yet now, O Lord, be merciful to bless
>   With more than these.
>
> Grant us the will to fashion as we feel,
> Grant us the strength to labour as we know,
> Grant us the purpose, ribb'd and edged with steel,
>   To strike the blow.
>
> Knowledge we ask not—knowledge thou hast lent,
> But, Lord, the will—there lies our bitter need,
> Give us to build above the deep intent
>   The deed, the deed.

Compassion

Being moved with compassion, he stretched forth his hand, and touched him, and saith unto him, I will; be thou made clean.

When the Lord saw her, he had compassion on her.—When he saw the multitudes, he was moved with compassion for them.

> And in his Face
> Divine Compassion visibly appeared.

The motive which Jesus always puts forward in his demand for brotherly kindness is that of compassion. Men are to help each other not from any calculation, or even from a sense of duty, but out of pure sympathy with their fellow-men. Jesus himself in his works of healing seems to have acted invariably from this motive of compassion.

The pity and sympathy of Jesus are unlike ours in having so much more intelligence and fellow-feeling in them. He understands men and women. After all, as Carlyle has pointed out in many places, it is this gift of tenderness and understanding, of sympathy, that gives the measure of our intellects; *e.g.* in *Biography* : " A loving heart is the beginning of all knowledge."

The nobler a soul is, the more objects of compassion it hath.

A man to be greatly good must imagine intensely and comprehensively; he must put himself in the place of another and of many others; the pains and pleasures of his species must become his own.

> Seek Love in the pity of others' woe,
>   In the gentle relief of another's care,
> In the darkness of night and the winter's snow,
>   In the naked and outcast, seek Love there !

> He prayeth well, who loveth well
>   Both man and bird and beast.
> He prayeth best, who loveth best
>   All things both great and small;
> For the dear God who loveth us,
>   He made and loveth all.

O God, who art Love, grant to thy children to bear one another's burdens in perfect good-will, that thy peace which passeth understanding may keep our hearts and minds in Christ Jesus our Lord.

Not Righteous but Sinners

The scribes of the Pharisees . . . said unto his disciples,
He eateth and drinketh with publicans and sinners. When
Jesus heard it, he saith unto them, They that are whole have
no need of a physician, but they that are sick : I came not to
call the righteous, but sinners.

The more one looks into those simple words, the more one
finds in them. Above all else, the evidence of the Master of
men. He is, one would think, on his defence ; by a dozen
simple words defence is transformed into an insidious and
devastating attack. Yet hardly an attack : merely the serpent
doubt set wandering for ever in the scribes' paradise of
certainty.

Mary, the great sinner, the woman of the town, heard Jesus
tell of the kingdom of God, how not they who were righteous,
but those who would turn and be changed, should enter into it.
She heard, as countless millions of sinners after her have heard,
and for ever will hear, the wonderful news of a loving God.
" There is more joy in heaven over one sinner that repenteth
than over ninety and nine that need no repentance." That,
when all is said and done, was the most wonderful declaration
of the nature of God that man has ever made. On the day
those words were said the world began to change, in a manner
not cognizable by science ; on that day forgiveness began to be
a faculty of the human soul.

> And all God's bells will carol soon
> For joy and glory and delight
> Of someone coming home to-night.

Without a fear and dread of self that will drive you to God
and Christ, without a taking in hand daily, and ever humbly
beginning anew, but not in your own strength, but in a despair
of self, which, if true, means an utter trust in God and Christ,
so utterly near you day and night—religion is fine talk, at least
it has not become fully alive.

> His love, not mine, the resting-place,
>   His truth, not mine, the tie.

> Just as I am, poor, wretched, blind,
> Sight, riches, healing of the mind,
> Yea, all I need in thee to find,
>   O Lamb of God, I come.

D

Faith

According to your faith be it done unto you.

With men it is impossible, but not with God : for all things are possible with God.—Jesus, seeing their faith.—I have not found so great faith, no, not in Israel.—O woman, great is thy faith : be it done unto thee even as thou wilt.—And Jesus answering saith unto them, Have faith in God. Verily I say unto you, Whosoever shall say unto this mountain, Be thou taken up and cast into the sea; and shall not doubt in his heart, but shall believe that what he saith cometh to pass; he shall have it.

Psychologists hold that what I can or cannot do depends not only on the desires and effort of my conscious self, but on the hopes, fears and convictions which have sunk deep into my subconscious mind. My idea of a living God cannot be a merely intellectual concept. According as I envisage his nature and his purpose, there will predominantly be connected with my idea of him feelings either of terror, shrinking and abasement, or of joyful adoration, love and trust. But once accept into my inmost self an idea fraught with emotion of either of these types, then by the fundamental laws of the nature of mind that idea must begin to *work*. It cannot but produce marked results—upon my whole outlook upon men and things, my temperament, my character, my nervous system and even my physical well-being. And those results will be directly proportionate to the extent to which it has penetrated my whole self.

Let us suppose a man to think of God in terms of Christ, to be convinced, that is, that God has a sublime purpose, is absolutely reliable, wholly loving; suppose further that he were to allow that vision to " work " in his subconscious mind. Should we not expect such a one to achieve enhancement of vitality, conquest of temptation, superiority to pain, triumph over circumstance ? For him vision would be translated into power.

It is of the essence of the Gospel of the Kingdom that we are not to measure our duty by past experience of the practicable, but are to estimate the possible by knowledge of our God-given duty.

Almighty God, lead us to know thee as the true home of our spirits, and through daily fellowship, with thee to come so to trust and love thee as our Father, that our lives may grow in power and fruitfulness, and no task or duty to which thou dost call us may seem impossible, through Jesus Christ, the captain and perfecter of our faith.

Need for Labourers

The harvest truly is plenteous, but the labourers are few. Pray ye therefore the Lord of the harvest, that he send forth labourers into his harvest.

Lift up your eyes, and look on the fields, that they are white already unto harvest.—When he saw the multitudes, he was moved with compassion for them, because they were distressed and scattered, as sheep not having a shepherd.

If I could show you these men and women, all the world over, in every stage of history, under every abuse of error, under every circumstance of failure, without hope, without help, without thanks, still obscurely fighting the lost fight of virtue, still clinging, in the brothel or on the scaffold, to some rag of honour, the poor jewel of their souls !

Oft when the Word is on me to deliver,
　Lifts the illusion and the truth lies bare;
Desert or throng, the city or the river,
　Melts in a lucid Paradise of air,—

Only like souls I see the folk thereunder,
　Bound who should conquer, slaves who should be kings,—
Hearing their one hope with an empty wonder,
　Sadly contented in a show of things.

　　　　Some life of men unblest
　　　　He knew. . . .

　　　　　　　Hearing oftentimes
　　　　The still, sad music of humanity.

Jesus saith, I stood in the midst of the world and in the flesh was I seen of them, and I found all men drunken, and none found I athirst among them, and my soul grieveth over the sons of men, because they are blind in their heart and see not.

Merciful God, who hast made all men for love, and willest that all should be saved and come to the knowledge of thy truth; have mercy upon those that know thee not; and so fetch them home, blessed Lord, to thy Son who was lifted up to draw all men unto him, that they may be numbered among thy faithful servants, and be made one flock under one shepherd.

Endurance

He that endureth to the end, the same shall be saved.

We call them blessed which endured.—Having patiently endured, he obtained the promise.—He endured, as seeing him who is invisible.—In everything commending ourselves, as ministers of God, in much patience, in afflictions, in necessities, in distresses, . . . in labours, in watchings, in fastings.

> Therefore we never flinch, but
> Even though our outward man be wasting away,
> Yet our inward man is being day by day renewed.

Manliness (in Spenser's *Faerie Queene*) is the quality of soul which frankly accepts the conditions in human life, of labour, of obedience, of effort, of unequal success; which does not quarrel with them or evade them, but takes for granted with unquestioning alacrity that man is called—by his call to high aims and destiny—to a continual struggle with difficulty, with pain, with evil, and makes it the point of honour not to be dismayed or wearied out by them.

> Yet I argue not
> Against Heav'n's hand or will, nor bate a jot
> Of heart or hope; but still bear up and steer
> Right onward.

> If you can make one heap of all your winnings
> And risk it on one turn of pitch-and-toss,
> And lose, and start again at your beginnings
> And never breathe a word about your loss;
> If you can force your heart and nerve and sinew
> To serve your turn long after they are gone,
> And so hold on when there is nothing in you
> Except the Will which says to them " Hold on." . . .

Whether we stumble or whether we fall, we must only think of rising again, and going on in our course.

Give me, O Lord, a steadfast heart, which no unworthy affection may drag downwards; give me an unconquered heart, which no tribulation can wear out; give me an upright heart, which no unworthy purpose may tempt aside. Bestow on me also, O Lord my God, understanding to know thee, diligence to seek thee, wisdom to find thee, and a faithfulness that may finally embrace thee.

Fatherly Care

Are not two sparrows sold for a farthing ? and not one of them
shall fall on the ground without your Father : but the very
hairs of your head are all numbered. Fear not therefore ;
ye are of more value than many sparrows.

I am persuaded, that neither death, nor life . . . shall be
able to separate us from the love of God, which is in Christ
Jesus our Lord.—The eternal God is thy dwelling place, and
underneath are the everlasting arms.—Like as a father pitieth
his children, so the Lord pitieth them that fear him.

Here then is the gist of Christianity for you in a single sentence : At the centre of the Universe there is That which is
more like a father's loving heart than like anything else we
know.

In its essence the Gospel is a call to make the experiment of
comradeship, the experiment of trusting the heart of things,
throwing self-care to the winds, in the sure and certain faith
that you will not be deserted, forsaken nor betrayed, and that
your ultimate interests are perfectly secure in the hands of the
Great Companion.

How can it possibly fail to steady the nerves, to cool the
fever, and appease the fret, if one be sensibly conscious that,
no matter what one's difficulties for the moment may appear
to be, one's life as a whole is in the keeping of a power whom
one can absolutely trust ?

> I bind unto myself to-day
>   The power of God to hold and lead,
> His eye to watch, his might to stay,
>   His ear to hearken to my need,
> The wisdom of my God to teach,
>   His hand to guide, his shield to ward,
> The word of God to give me speech,
>   His heavenly host to be my guard.

Set free, O Lord, the souls of thy servants from all restless-
ness and anxiety ; give us that peace and power which flow
from thee ; and keep us in all perplexities and distresses from
any fear or faithlessness ; that so, upheld by thy strength and
stayed on the rock of thy faithfulness, through storm and stress
we may abide in thee.

Confession

Everyone therefore who shall confess me before men, him will I also confess before my Father which is in heaven.

Whosoever shall be ashamed of me and of my words in this adulterous and sinful generation, the Son of man also shall be ashamed of him, when he cometh in the glory of his Father with the holy angels.—I have not hid thy righteousness within my heart; I have declared thy faithfulness and thy salvation : I have not concealed thy lovingkindness and thy truth from the great congregation.—I am not ashamed of the gospel : for it is the power of God unto salvation to everyone that believeth.

> Servant of God, well done, well hast thou fought
> The better fight, who single hast maintained
> Against revolted multitudes the cause
> Of Truth, in word mightier than they in Armes;
> And for the testimonie of Truth hast borne
> Universal reproach, far worse to beare
> Than violence; for this was all thy care
> To stand approv'd in sight of God, though Worlds
> Judg'd thee perverse.

Surely to every good and peaceable man it must in nature needs be a hateful thing to be the displeaser and molester of thousands . . . But when God commands us to take the trumpet and blow a dolorous or jarring blast, it lies not in man's will what he shall say, or what he shall conceal.

> Send us this day amongst our fellows,
> Held every moment in thine own strong friendship,
> To be for thee, triumphantly,
> The heralds of thy Will, thy Word,
> Thy generous Love, thy Hope, thy Joy,
> Thy Might, thy Purity, thy Beauty.

O Heavenly Father, the Father of all wisdom, understanding and true strength, look mercifully upon me and send thy Holy Spirit into my breast; that when I must join' to fight in the field for the glory of thy Holy Name, then I, being strengthened with the defence of thy right hand, may manfully stand in the confession of thy faith, and of thy truth, and continue in the same unto the end of my life.

An Uncalculating Devotion

Whosoever he be of you that renounceth not all that he hath, he cannot be my disciple.

He that loveth father or mother more than me is not worthy of me; and he that loveth son or daughter more than me is not worthy of me. And he that doth not take his cross and follow after me is not worthy of me.

Above the upturned faces of the broken-hearted men and women rose the calm, set features of Garibaldi, lit up with that serene and simple regard of fortitude and faith which gave him power to lead the feeble multitudes of mortal men. . . . The sonorous, thrilling voice was heard almost to the outskirts of the vast crowd:
" I am going out from Rome. . . . I offer neither pay, nor quarters, nor provisions; I offer hunger, thirst, forced marches, battles and death. Let him who loves his country in his heart and not with his lips only, follow me."

They grudged no sacrifice however unfruitful and shrank from no ordeal however destructive. No attack, however forlorn, however fatal, found them without ardour. No slaughter however desolating prevented them from returning to the charge. No physical conditions however severe deprived their commanders of their obedience and loyalty. Unconquerable except by death, which they had conquered, they have set up a monument of native virtue which will command the wonder, the reverence and the gratitude of our people as long as we endure as a nation among men.

Maturus and Sanctus passed again through every torment in the amphitheatre. . . . They endured again the customary running of the gauntlet and the violence of the wild beasts, and everything which the furious people called for or desired. . . . But even thus they did not hear a word from Sanctus except the confession which he had uttered from the beginning. These, then, after their life had continued for a long time through the great conflict, were at last sacrificed, having been made throughout that day a spectacle to the world.

We are exceedingly frail, and indisposed to every virtuous and gallant undertaking. Strengthen our weakness, we beseech thee, O Lord, that we may do valiantly in this spiritual war; help us against our own negligence and cowardice, and defend us from the treachery of our unfaithful hearts.

The Secret of Life

He that findeth his life shall lose it; and he that loseth his life for my sake shall find it.

The law of self-sacrifice lies at the very heart of the Christian message. The true disciple must forget himself utterly in his absolute loyalty to the will of God. He must renounce everything that seems to make life desirable, and, if need be, life itself. But this renunciation is the necessary condition of a greater good. By denying himself a man becomes capable of the service of God, and only in this service can he truly fulfil himself.

The heart of man is so constituted that its fulness comes of spending. When we serve we rule. When we give we have. When we surrender ourselves we are victors. We are most ourselves when we lose sight of ourselves.

In heroism, we feel, life's supreme mystery is hidden. No matter what a man's frailties otherwise may be, if he be willing to risk death, and still more if he suffer it heroically in the service he has chosen, the fact consecrates him for ever. Inferior to ourselves in this or that way, if yet we cling to life, and he is able " to fling it away like a flower " as caring nothing for it, we account him in the deepest way our born superior. Each of us in his own person feels that a high-hearted indifference to life would expiate all his shortcomings.

The metaphysical mystery, that he who feeds on death that feeds on men possesses life supereminently and meets best the demands of the universe, is the truth of which asceticism has been the faithful champion. The folly of the cross, so inexplicable by the intellect, has yet its indestructible vital meaning. Naturalistic optimism is mere syllabub and sponge-cake in comparison.

> Draw near, my friends; and let your thoughts be high;
>   Great hearts are glad when it is time to give;
> Life is no life to him that dares not die,
>   And death no death to him that dares to live.

O God, who hast made us so that only those who do not live in themselves know what life is, grant that in spending ourselves freely we may enter into fulness of life.

Jesus' Mission

And Jesus answered and said unto them, Go your way and tell John the things which ye do hear and see : the blind receive their sight, and the lame walk, the lepers are cleansed, and the deaf hear, and the dead are raised up, and the poor have good tidings preached to them.

And he opened the book, and found the place where it was written, The Spirit of the Lord is upon me, because he anointed me to preach good tidings to the poor : he hath sent me to proclaim release to the captives, and recovering of sight to the blind, to set at liberty them that are bruised. . . . And he began to say unto them, To-day hath this scripture been fulfilled in your ears.—In the wilderness shall waters break out, and streams in the desert. And the glowing sand shall become a pool, and the thirsty ground springs of water.—And a man shall be as an hiding place from the wind, and a covert from the tempest; as rivers of water in a dry place, as the shadow of a great rock in a weary land.

It is not only necessary that we should know that God became man, it is also necessary that we should know what kind of man he became.

> For Mercy has a human heart,
> Pity a human face,
> And Love, the human form divine,
> And Peace, the human dress.

Practically every one of the great recorded deeds of Jesus is like a revelation of a higher and happier world. The dispelling of disease of body and mind, the control of the powers of nature that work tragedy in human life . . . what are they but manifestations of the life that shall be perfected in heaven, when the long course of man's history shall culminate at last in reaching its home in that infinite ocean of love and life which we call God ? So they are, one and all, fragments of heaven and " intimations of immortality," as the wild spring flowers are prophecies and fragments of the splendour of the high summer-time.

O God, we would live to-day by thy life, be moved by thy will, speak the words of thy love unto men, step clear of this half-existence into life abundant of service for thee.

Rest

No one knoweth the . . . Father, save the Son, and he to whomsoever the Son willeth to reveal him. Come unto me, all ye that labour and are heavy laden, and I will give you rest. Take my yoke upon you, and learn of me; for I am meek and lowly in heart : and ye shall find rest unto your souls.

No one ever lived who accomplished a work so great as that of Jesus Christ. No one ever bore the burden of so tremendous a mission; yet the impression conveyed by his life is one of repose and tranquillity. So deep and unshakable was his confidence in the God whom he knew as Father that he could invite the whole world to come and share his rest.

The recurrence of the name Father unveils the secret of his being. His heart is at rest in God.

There is no rest for the heart of man save in God, who made him for himself. But how shall we rest in God? By giving ourselves wholly to him. If you give yourself by halves, you cannot find full rest—there will ever be a lurking disquiet in that half which is withheld; and for this reason it is that so few Christians attain to a full, steadfast, unchanging peace— they do not seek rest in God only, or give themselves up to him without reserve. True rest is as unchanging as God himself. It stills all passion, restrains the imagination, steadies the mind, controls all wavering; it endures alike in the time of tribulation and in the time of wealth; in temptation and trial, as when the world shines brightly on us. Such words may seem ex- aggeration to those who have not tried it; but the saints will tell you otherwise. St. Paul will tell you of a peace which passeth understanding; Jesus Christ tells you of his peace which the world can neither give nor take away.

> I ask not that false calm which many feign,
> And call that peace which is a dearth of pain.
> True calm doth quiver like the calmest star;
> It is that white where all the colours are;
> And for its very vestibule doth own
> The tree of Jesus and the pyre of Joan.

Let the hands or the head be at labour, the heart ought nevertheless to rest in God.

Bless us, O God, with the vision of thy Being and beauty, that in the joy of thy strength we may work without haste and without sloth; through Jesus Christ our Lord.

The Friendship of Christ

And he appointed twelve, that they might be with him.

Ye are they which have continued with me in my temptations.—With desire I have desired to eat this passover with you before I suffer.—I have called you friends; for all things that I heard from my Father I have made known unto you.— Having loved his own which were in the world, he loved them unto the end.

The Gospel began with friendship, and we know from common life what that is, and how it works. In this easier and more careless intercourse, when the mind is off guard, it is receiving a host of unnoticed impressions, which in the long run may have extraordinary influence. Pleasant and easy-going, a perpetual source of interest and rest of mind, the friendship continues, till we find to our surprise that we are changed. Stage by stage, as one comes to know one's friend, one lives the other man's life, sees and feels things as he does, and wakes up to find oneself, as it were, remade by the other's personality.

> Learned his great language, caught his clear accents.

If it can be said of the transforming influence of companionship with nature :

> And she shall lean her ear
> In many a secret place
> Where rivulets dance their wayward round,
> And beauty born of murmuring sound
> Shall pass into her face,—

and of the comradeship of the home (the priest Caponsacchi is speaking) :

> I do but play with an imagined life
> Of who, unfettered by a vow, unblessed
> By the higher call—since you will have it so—
> Leads it companioned by the woman there.
> To live, and see her learn, and learn by her. . . .
> To have to do with nothing but the true,
> The good, the eternal—and these, not alone
> In the main current of the general life,
> But small experiences of every day,
> Concerns of the particular hearth and home,—

what may not that man become who holds daily company with Christ ?

Draw us, O Lord, into such intimate fellowship with thyself, and let thy words which are spirit and life so abide in us, that we may be changed in heart and mind and may daily become more like thee, our Master and Friend.

The Secret of Goodness

Make the tree good.

There is no good tree that bringeth forth corrupt fruit; nor again a corrupt tree that bringeth forth good fruit. . . . For of thorns men do not gather figs, nor of a bramble bush gather they grapes. The good man out of the good treasure of his heart bringeth forth that which is good; and the evil man out of the evil treasure bringeth forth that which is evil : for out of the abundance of the heart his mouth speaketh.

Most rules of life undertake to regulate behaviour. But when Christianity sums up its rule of life, it addresses itself to the feelings or affections. It states its requirements in terms of a complete transformation of the instincts.

The purpose of Jesus, as Paul discerned, was not to enforce a rule that must be followed with labour and difficulty, but to impart a spirit which would take the place of law. The Christian character at its finest has always answered to this requirement of Jesus, and this has been the secret of its charm. We can feel that its virtues are not the result of painful effort, but are the outflow of an inner spring. They are the very nature of the man, and he exercises them unconsciously, and without effort or reserve.

> The churl in spirit, howe'er he veil
>   His want in forms for fashion's sake,
>   Will let his coltish nature break
> At seasons through the gilded pale :
>
> For who can always act ? but he,
>   To whom a thousand memories call,
>   Not being less but more than all
> The gentleness he seem'd to be.
>
> Best seem'd the thing he was, and join'd
>   Each office of the social hour
>   To noble manners, as the flower
> And native growth of noble mind.

Christianity conceives of the transformation of the self, not through the mere destruction of the narrow and corrupt flesh which alienates it from the true life, but by the simple yet intensely positive devotion of the self to a new task.

Almighty God, unto whom all hearts be open, all desires known, and from whom no secrets are hid; cleanse the thoughts of our hearts by the inspiration of thy Holy Spirit, that we may perfectly love thee, and worthily magnify thy holy Name.

The Parables of Seed and Growth

And he taught them many things in parables.

Behold, the sower went forth to sow : and it came to pass, as he sowed, some seed fell by the wayside. . . . And other fell among the thorns. . . . And others fell into the good ground, and yielded fruit.—So is the kingdom of God, as if a man should cast seed upon the earth; and should sleep and rise night and day, and the seed should spring up and grow, he knoweth not how. The earth beareth fruit of herself; first the blade, then the ear, then the full corn in the ear.—How shall we liken the kingdom of God ? . . . It is like a grain of mustard seed, which, when it is sown upon the earth, though it be less than all the seeds that are upon the earth, yet when it is sown, groweth up, and becometh greater than all the herbs.

Everywhere were parables : the common happenings were full of meaning : they had a message of God's kingdom for those who had eyes to see. It is in this constant atmosphere of communion with God through the universal sacrament of his works that Jesus lives and teaches.

Jesus saith, Ye ask who are those that draw us to the kingdom, if the kingdom is in heaven ? The fowls of the air, and all the beasts that are under the earth or upon the earth, and the fishes of the sea, these are they which draw you, and the kingdom of heaven is within you, and whoever shall know himself shall find it.

> Even such a shell the universe itself
> Is to the ear of Faith; and there are times,
> I doubt not, when to you it doth impart
> Authentic tidings of invisible things.

The crucial reference for the teaching of " the mystery of the kingdom of God " is the fourth chapter of Mark. If it be accepted that Mark's gospel is based upon the reminiscences of Peter, the fundamental importance of that chapter, in itself obvious, is immeasurably enhanced. There is singularly little of Jesus' teaching in Mark's gospel; and the significance of the one chapter that is wholly devoted to it is increased accordingly. We may conclude that Peter believed that the real essence of Jesus' message was contained therein.

O Lord, by the Spirit, move in our very beings, that we may see thee in everything that is, that we may hear thy voice speaking more clearly than all voices, and feel thy presence in every movement and experience.

Joy

The kingdom of heaven is like unto a treasure hidden in the field; which a man found, and hid; and in his joy he goeth and selleth all that he hath, and buyeth that field.

And Jesus said unto them, Can the sons of the bride-chamber fast, while the bridegroom is with them ?—Your sorrow shall be turned into joy.—Ask and ye shall receive, that your joy may be fulfilled.—The abundance of their joy.—On whom, though now ye see him not, yet believing, ye rejoice greatly with joy unspeakable.—And the ransomed of the Lord shall return, and come with singing unto Zion; and everlasting joy shall be upon their heads : they shall obtain gladness and joy, and sorrow and sighing shall flee away.

The true realism, always and everywhere, is that of the poets : to find out where joy resides, and give it a voice far beyond singing. For to miss the joy is to miss all. In the joy of the actors lies the sense of any action.

The divinely intended end of our life is joy overflowing and infinite, a joy closely connected with a noble asceticism. There is a wholesome, a strengthening *zest* attached to all action which is right and appropriate for the agent. Now there is no zest comparable to the zest, the expansion, the joy brought to the soul by God and the soul's close union with him.

Love directed towards the eternal and infinite feeds the mind with pure joy, and is free from all sadness.

The blessed Francis ever made it his highest and chief study apart from prayer and the Divine office, to have continually spiritual joy, both inwardly and outwardly; and this likewise he particularly loved in his brothers, often rebuking them for sadness and for showing their grief. And he was wont to say to them, " Since this spiritual joy comes of cleanness of heart and the purity of continual prayer, ye should seek above all to acquire and conserve these two things, that ye may possess, within and without, that joy."

If I have faltered more or less
In my great task of happiness. . . .

Make us joyful with gladness unforced,
Contagious, abounding,
That all whom we meet may be kindled, from us,
With thy fire of joy.

Energy of Mind

The kingdom of heaven is like unto a man that is a merchant seeking goodly pearls : and having found one pearl of great price, he went and sold all that he had, and bought it.

The kingdom of heaven suffereth violence, and men of violence take it by force.—Jesus said unto him, No man, having put his hand to the plough, and looking back, is fit for the kingdom of God.

It is worth while to look at the type of character which Jesus admires. How many of the parables turn on energy ? Thus the parable of the talents turns on energetic thinking and decisive action; and these are the things that Jesus admires—in the widow who *will* have justice; in the virgins who thought ahead and brought extra oil; in the vigorous man who found the treasure and made sure of it; in the friend at midnight, who hammered, hammered, hammered till he got his loaves; in the man who will hack off his hand to enter into life. On the other side, he is always against the life of drift, the half-thought-out life. There they were, he says, in the days of Noah, eating, drinking, marrying, dreaming—and the flood came and destroyed them. There is the person who everlastingly *says* and does not *do*, who promises to work and does not work, who receives a new idea with enthusiasm but has not depth enough of nature for it to root itself, who builds on sand, the sort that compromises, that tries to serve God and mammon, all the practical half-and-half people. It is energy of mind that he calls for—either with me or against me.

All other faults or deficiencies Christ could tolerate, but he could have neither part nor lot with men destitute of enthusiasm.

Strong passions awaken the faculties. They suffer not a particle of the man to be lost.

Breathe on me with that breath which infuses energy and kindles fervour. In asking for fervour, I ask for all that I can need. I am asking for faith, hope, and charity in their most heavenly exercise; I am asking for that loyal perception of duty which follows on yearning affection; I am asking for sanctity, peace and joy, all at once. I am asking for thyself. Enter my heart, and fill it with fervour by filling it with thee.

The Veil of the Commonplace

Is not this the carpenter, the son of Mary, and brother of James, and Joses, and Judas, and Simon ? and are not his sisters here with us ?

And she brought forth her firstborn son; and she . . . laid him in a manger, because there was no room for them in the inn.—See that ye despise not one of these little ones; for I say unto you, that in heaven their angels do always behold the face of my Father which is in heaven.—And Jacob awaked out of his sleep, and he said, Surely the Lord is in this place; and I knew it not.

> The angels keep their ancient places;—
>   Turn but a stone and start a wing !
> 'Tis ye, 'tis your estrangèd faces,
>   That miss the many-splendoured thing.
>
> But (when so sad thou canst not sadder)
>   Cry and upon thy so sore loss
> Shall shine the traffic of Jacob's ladder
>   Pitched betwixt Heaven and Charing Cross.
>
> Yea, in the night, my soul, my daughter,
>   Cry—clinging Heaven by the hems;
> And lo, Christ walking on the water,
>   Not of Gennesareth, but Thames !
>
> An idle poet, here and there,
>   Looks round him; but, for all the rest,
> The world, unfathomably fair,
>   Is duller than a witling's jest.
> Love wakes men, once a lifetime each;
>   They lift their heavy lids, and look;
> And lo, what one sweet page can teach,
>   They read with joy, then shut the book.
>
> So let me feel thy presence day by day
>   In wind and sod,
> That every bush I meet upon the way
>   Shall glow with God.
>
> So let thy Spirit kindle my desire,
>   Self to deny,
> That every common deed shall flame with fire
>   As doth thy sky.

Thou art the Christ

Peter answereth and saith unto him, Thou art the Christ.

Simon Peter answered him, Lord, to whom shall we go ?
Thou hast the words of eternal life.—A man shall be as an
hiding place from the wind, and a covert from the tempest; as
rivers of water in a dry place, as the shadow of a great rock in a
weary land.—Thomas answered and said unto him, My Lord
and my God.

We do not know which first to designate great, whether the
lofty flight of the disciples who renounce the Jewish standard,
quash the verdict of hierarchs, leap over popular opinion, find
the insignificant and the down-trodden lofty and divine, because
spiritually to spiritual eyes it is something high and remains
something divine; or that personality of Jesus, which compels
such weak disciples, even under the paralyzing influence of all
external facts, distinctly and simply and nobly to mirror back
the total impression of his ministry.

He makes upon us a unique impression, the impression that
in him, as in none other, God has come to us, to disclose to us
his inmost heart to condemn our sin, to call us to his service,
and to create within us the life that is life indeed.

The originality of Christianity consists not so much in its
single doctrines, or even in its teaching as a whole, as in its
revelation, through the person and example of its Founder, of
the altogether unsuspected depth and inexhaustibleness of
human Personality.

> Jesu, thou Joy of loving hearts,
> Thou Fount of life, thou Light of men,
> From the best bliss that earth imparts
> We turn unfilled to thee again.

Thou art the King of Glory :   O Christ.
Thou art the everlasting Son of the Father.
When thou tookest upon thee to deliver man,
Thou didst not abhor the Virgin's womb.
When thou hadst overcome the sharpness of death,
Thou didst open the kingdom of heaven to all believers.

E

The Son of Man must Suffer

And he began to teach them, that the Son of man must suffer many things.

He was despised, and rejected of men; a man of sorrows, and acquainted with grief. . . . He shall see of the travail of his soul, and shall be satisfied. . . . Therefore will I divide him a portion with the great . . . because he poured out his soul unto death.

Victory out of utter defeat as the inmost secret of God's plan —even if our dull minds respond to that amazing vision of Isaiah and recognize its inspiration, what would it have been to one whose ears were attuned as no man's have ever been to hear the secret voice of God?

It is laid in the unalterable constitution of things—none can aspire to act greatly but those who are of force greatly to suffer.

Not one of the philosophers or systems before Christ had effectually escaped falling either into Pessimism, seeing the end of life as trouble and weariness, and seeking to escape from it into some aloofness or some Nirvana; or into Optimism, ignoring or explaining away that suffering and trial which, as our first experience and as our last, surround us on every side. But with him, and alone with him and those who still learn and live from and by him, there is the union of the clearest, keenest sense of all the mysterious depth and breadth and length and height of human sadness, suffering, and sin, and, in spite of this and through this and at the end of this, a note of conquest and of triumphant joy. And here, as elsewhere in Christianity, this is achieved not by some artificial, facile juxtaposition : but all its pain gets fully faced and willed, gets taken up into the conscious life. Suffering thus becomes the highest form of action, a divinely potent means of satisfaction, recovery, and enlargement for the soul—the soul with its mysteriously great consciousness of pettiness and sin, and its immense capacity for joy in self-donation.

Almighty God, who hast shown us in the life and teaching of thy Son the true way of blessedness, thou hast also showed us in his suffering and death that the path of love may lead to the Cross, and the reward of faithfulness may be a crown of thorns. Give us grace to learn these hard lessons. May we take up our cross and follow Christ, in the strength of patience and the constancy of faith; and see even in our darkest hour of trial and anguish the shining of the eternal light.

Discipleship

If any man would come after me, let him deny himself and take up his cross, and follow me.

A disciple is not above his master, nor a servant above his lord. It is enough for the disciple that he be as his master, and the servant as his lord.

The voice of the true ethic is dangerous for the happy when they have the courage to listen to it. For them there is no quenching of the irrational fire which glows in it. It challenges them in an attempt to lead them away from the natural road, and to see whether it can make them the adventurers of self-sacrifice, of whom the world has too few. The idea that men should ever be favoured by being free from the responsibilities of self-sacrifice as men for men is foreign to this ethic. Open your eyes and look for some man, or some work for the sake of men, which needs a little time, a little friendship, a little sympathy, a little sociability, a little human toil. Search and see if there is not some place where you may invest your humanity.

He comes to us as of old, by the lakeside, he came to those men who knew him not. He speaks to us the same words, "Follow thou me!" and sets us to the tasks which he has to fulfil for our time. He commands. And to those who obey him, he will reveal himself in the toils, the conflicts, the sufferings which they shall pass through in his fellowship, and, as an ineffable mystery, they shall learn in their own experience who he is.

Christianity began in something that happened, in a deed that was done, in a life that was lived. In the beginning was the deed : go thou and do likewise. So presented, Christianity is not perplexing; but quite the most convincing religion ever offered to the intellect or the heart.

> Life with its path before us lies;
> Christ is the way and Christ the prize.

If ever we faint under any appointed cross and say "It is too hard to bear," may we look to the steps of the Man of Sorrows toiling on to Calvary, and pass freely into thy hand, and become one with him and thee. Dedicate us to the joyful service of thy will; and own us as thy children in time and in eternity.

Courage

When the days were well-nigh come that he should be received up, he stedfastly set his face to go to Jerusalem.

And he said unto them, Why are ye fearful ? Have ye not yet faith ?—Be not afraid of them which kill the body, but are not able to kill the soul.—If any man would come after me, let him deny himself, and take up his cross, and follow me.— When they beheld the boldness of Peter and John . . . they marvelled; and they took knowledge of them, that they had been with Jesus.

Jesus, as much as pagan teachers, insists on courage as the primary virtue. The great difference between them is not in their estimate of courage, or even in the kind of courage they value, but in the motive to which they trace it. For Jesus courage is not a matter of physical constitution, or for that part a purely moral quality, but the expression of faith in God. In the confidence that God is supporting them men can meet all circumstances fearlessly, knowing that they will overcome the world. Courage is thus a vital element not merely in the ethic of Jesus but in his religion.

> Jesus, whose lot with us was cast,
> Who saw it out, from first to last :
> Patient and fearless, tender, true,
> Carpenter, vagabond, felon, Jew ;
> Who, as your hour neared, did not fail—
> The world's fate trembling in the scale—
> With your half-hearted band to dine,
> And chat across the bread and wine ;
> Then went out firm to face the end,
> Alone, without a single friend :
> Who felt, as your last words confessed,
> Wrung from a proud, unflinching breast
> By hours of dull, ignoble pain,
> Your whole life's fight was fought in vain :
> Would I could win and keep and feel
> That heart of love, that spirit of steel.

We pray thee to-day for thine own strong courage. Give us courage to combat thy enemies and to suffer in thy cause. Spur us this day to challenge the grim realities of pain, disease, injustice and sin, and by gallant service to conquer these thy foes.

Work and Enjoyment

Howbeit in this rejoice not, that the spirits are subject unto you; but rejoice that your names are written in heaven.

The very greatest achievements fall below the assurance, at once humble and proud, of resting for time and eternity under the Fatherly care of God.

Ambition and duty, all use of conscious freedom, all *work*, in short, develops of itself an inner opposition or spiritual check-age. For this loss of margin, as the artificial self becomes identified with its own assumptions and objects, is a progressive impoverishment. Into the midst of all effort, dutiful or otherwise, there must fall, soon or late, a sense of the aimlessness of work, a consciousness of moral wear and tear in the determined pursuit of objects whose value is not wholly convincing. And this new-born need turns naturally toward some object whose value is convincing without any effort, toward *enjoyment* in some form or other. Pleasure, recreation, friendship, companionship, beauty—all these reunite a man with his natural appreciation. *And worship is the whole which includes them all.*

Sound and activity and pleasures all cease to be significant for men who never withdraw from them; such men have no scale of values and become incapable of appreciation.

Religion even, more than all other convictions that claim correspondence with the real, begins and proceeds and ends with the Given—with existences, realities, which environ and penetrate us, and which we have always anew to capture and to combine, to fathom and to apprehend.

Most men seem to live and die, hardly touched by the sense, which alone makes us fully awake human beings, of our little finitude touched and kept restless, and yet also rested, by the Infinite, by God our living origin and home.

Teach us, gracious God, so to open our hearts to thee that the light and warmth of thy love may flood our beings as the flowers drink in the light and warmth of the sun; so to worship and adore thee, to rest and rejoice in thy Presence, that through such communion our life may be renewed at its deepest source and new creative impulses come to birth.

The Better Part

But Martha was cumbered about much serving; and she came up to him, and said, Lord, dost thou not care that my sister did leave me to serve alone ? bid her therefore that she help me. But the Lord answered and said unto her, Martha, Martha, thou art anxious and troubled about many things : but one thing is needful : for Mary hath chosen the good part, which shall not be taken away from her.

Fénelon pointed out to the Duc de Chevreuse how over-burdened and how racketed and distracted was the Duke's life, outside of his direct and deliberate praying; and how greatly that overburdenedness, when out of prayer, damaged his recollection when in prayer. Fénelon advised the Duke to begin his day with quietly running through in his mind the things that he would probably have to do during that coming day. That he should then and there reduce the number of such things as much as was wisely possible ; and that, when he came to the actual doing of these things, he should clip his action of all unnecessary detail and development. In this way he would succeed in placing each action within a circumambient air of leisure—of leisure for the spirit of prayer and peace. This would be like the ordering of a wise gardener, who carefully sees to it that the young trees he plants have sufficient spaces each from the other—have sufficient air in which to grow and expand.

Man attains in religion, as truly as elsewhere—once given his whole-hearted striving—in proportion as he seeks not too directly, not feverishly and strainingly, but in a largely sub-conscious, waiting, genial, expansive, endlessly patient, sunny manner.

> Nor less I deem that there are Powers
>   Which of themselves our minds impress ;
> That we can feed this mind of ours
>   In a wise passiveness.
>
> Think you, 'mid all this mighty sum
>   Of things for ever speaking,
> That nothing of itself will come,
>   But we must still be seeking ?

Bestow on us, O Lord, a growing understanding of the true values of life; increase our powers of insight and enlarge our capacity for appreciation, and grant to us that waiting and receptive attitude of soul, wherein lie the hidden springs of high endeavour and fruitful action.

Sincerity

There is nothing covered up, that shall not be revealed : and hid, that shall not be known.

Thy Father which seeth in secret.—This is the message which we have heard from him, and announce unto you, that God is light, and in him is no darkness at all. If we say that we have fellowship with him, and walk in the darkness, we lie, and do not the truth : but if we walk in the light, as he is in the light, we have fellowship one with another.—Let us keep the feast . . . with the unleavened bread of sincerity and truth.

Sincerity, as Jesus conceives it, implies that all thoughts and motives can fully bear the light.

Jesus' emphatic, incisive warning against hypocrisy designates not so much the crude sort of hypocrisy which consists in pretending to the direct opposite of what is actually believed, as the more subtle inner untruthfulness in which the outward act leaves the basis of the nature indifferent, and occupation with divine things is united with cunning, with the lust of power, and with selfishness.

Sincerity, a deep, great, genuine sincerity, is the first characteristic of all men in any way heroic.

There is the mystery of veracity : " Naked came I into the world "—whoever first said that, possessed this mystery. My own bare entity must fight the battle—shams cannot save me.

We thank thee, to-day,
That our lives lie open and plain
To thy piercing vision,
That we face unsheltered
Thyself and our own true selves.
We thank thee that thus all illusion
Is daily rent from our souls,
So that, morning by morning,
We know ourselves to be mean and filthy and sin-smeared,
For ever unworthy of thine unwearying love,
For ever dependent, in weakness and shame,
On thy power, thy cleanness, thy grace.

O Holy Lord God, who searchest the hearts and triest the reins of the children of men, cleanse me from all hypocrisy and give me truth in the inward parts, that being pure in heart I may see thee in thy kingdom.

Having and Being

A man's life consisteth not in the abundance of the things which he possesseth.

God said unto him, Thou foolish one, this night is thy soul required of thee; and the things which thou hast prepared, whose shall they be? So is he that layeth up treasure for himself, and is not rich toward God.—What is a man profited, if he gain the whole world, and lose or forfeit his own self?—Is not the life more than the food, and the body than the raiment?

A deeper contrast is scarcely to be found than between the view of life which thinks of it primarily as possessive and that which looks on it as creative; between the state of mind which is set on acquisition and that for which life means the adventure of man's soul in the universe.

Society has undoubtedly got to pass toward some newer and better equilibrium, and the distribution of wealth has doubtless slowly got to change. But to expect that such changes will make any genuine vital difference on a large scale to the lives of our descendants would be a great mistake. The solid meaning of life is always the same eternal thing—the marriage, namely, of some unhabitual ideal, however special, with some fidelity, courage and endurance; with some man's or woman's pains. And, whatever or wherever life may be, there will always be the chance for that marriage to take place.

I gave up the life of the conventional world, recognizing it to be no life, but a parody on life, which its superfluities simply keep us from comprehending.

The common cognomen of this world among the misguided and superstitious is " a vale of tears," from which we are to be redeemed by a certain arbitrary interposition of God and taken to heaven. What a little, circumscribed, straitened notion! Call the world if you please " The vale of soul-making."

> I count life just a stuff
> To try the soul's strength on, educe the man.

O Lord, our Father, free our souls from attachment to the things of this world; let us not be brought into subjection to the lust of the flesh, the lust of the eyes and the vainglory of life; and enable us as thy free sons to serve thee in the world.

The Kingdom God's Gift

It is your Father's good pleasure to give you the kingdom.

So is the kingdom of God, as if a man should cast seed upon the earth; and should sleep and rise night and day, and the seed should spring up and grow, he knoweth not how.—Of that day and hour knoweth no one . . . neither the Son, but the Father only.

It is commonly assumed that men themselves must bring the Kingdom into being. The very programme of Christianity, as it is often understood, is to establish the Kingdom of God on earth by the concentrated effort of all good men. To Jesus this conception would have been meaningless, and even repellent. The Kingdom, as he knew it, was God's, and men could no more establish it than they could make the sun rise in heaven. His attitude was always that of trust in a divine power and wisdom which will accomplish for us what we cannot do ourselves. This did not mean that men were to stand by passively until God fulfilled his promise, but that they could count on God.

Jesus does not speak of the Kingdom of God as of something that comes into existence through a development of human society, but as of something which is brought about by God. In his thought the ethical activity of man is only like a powerful prayer to God, that he may cause the Kingdom to appear without delay. There is a deep significance in the fact that Jesus does not establish the organic connection, which to us seems so natural, between the ethical acts of men and the realization of the Kingdom of God. It signifies that we are to be ethical, not in the expectation of thereby fulfilling some purpose, but from inward necessity, so as to enter into his will.

O God of unchangeable power and eternal light, look favourably on thy whole Church, that wonderful and sacred mystery; and by the tranquil operation of thy perpetual providence carry out the work of man's salvation : and let the whole world feel and see that things which were cast down are being raised up : that those which had grown old are being made new; and that all things are returning to perfection, through him from whom they took their origin, even our Lord Jesus Christ.

Value of the Individual

What man of you, having a hundred sheep, and having lost one of them, doth not leave the ninety and nine in the wilderness, and go after that which is lost, until he find it ? . . . Even so there shall be joy in heaven over one sinner that repenteth.

Are not two sparrows sold for a farthing ? and not one of them shall fall on the ground without your Father. . . . Ye are of more value than many sparrows.—See that ye despise not one of these little ones ; for I say unto you, that in heaven their angels do always behold the face of my Father which is in heaven.

When Jesus seeks to determine our duty to our fellow-men he sets out from the conviction that every soul has a value in the sight of God. He does not think in terms of masses but in terms of the individual. His primary interest is not that of making the world better, for this will be accomplished by God himself, when he brings in the Kingdom, but that of fostering an active goodness in men and women. The opportunity is given us, in our human relations, of acting as God himsel^f does, and of thus becoming his children.

The Christian ethos alone, in virtue of its belief in a personal God, possesses an idea of personality and individuality which has a metaphysical basis and is proof against every attack of naturalism or pessimism. Only the personality which, transcending the purely natural, comes into existence through the union of the will and of the whole being with God is raised above the finite and can defy it.

Every individual, as modern psychology and educational experience are coming more and more to recognize, is unique. Each must develop according to the law of his own nature ; he must be good and happy in his own characteristic way. As every true teacher knows, no one can transfer any vital experience or knowledge directly to another. What that other learns he will inevitably and rightly clothe and colour with his own habits of thought, feeling and will and the qualities of his own unshared experiences. The starting-point of right relations with our fellow-men is the recognition that each is a unique individual, that each has his peculiar and irreplaceable contribution to make to fulfilment of God's purpose in the world.

Teach us, O God, to look upon each of our fellow-men with the eyes of Christ, to recognize in each the uniqueness of his individuality and of the contribution which he may make to thy kingdom, and to think of him as the object of thy Fatherly regard and of thy redeeming love.

The Reversal of Human Judgment

Ye are they that justify yourselves in the sight of men; but God knoweth your hearts : for that which is exalted among men is an abomination in the sight of God.

Verily I say unto you, that the publicans and the harlots go into the kingdom of God before you.—Every one that exalteth himself shall be humbled; and he that humbleth himself shall be exalted.—God chose the weak things of the world, that he might put to shame the things that are strong; and the base things of the world, and the things that are despised, did God choose, yea and the things that are not, that he might bring to nought the things that are.

The summary of the new teaching in the Sermon on the Mount is prefaced by the Beatitudes, in which Jesus portrays the kind of man who will find entrance into the Kingdom. Just as this age produces the character which is fitted to thrive in it— the self-centred, aggressive, worldly-minded man—so the coming age will require men of a temper altogether different. Such men alone will find themselves at home in the new conditions. All values will be completely changed, so that qualities which have hitherto been cherished will become useless. The first will be last and the last first.

As for me, my bed is made : I am against bigness and greatness in all their forms, and with the invisible molecular moral forces that work from individual to individual, stealing in through the crannies of the world like so many soft rootlets, or like the capillary oozing of water, and yet rending the hardest monuments of man's pride, if you give them time. I am against all big organizations as such, national ones first and foremost; against all big successes and big results; and in favour of the eternal forces of truth which always work in the individual and immediately unsuccessful way, under-dogs always, till history comes, after they are long dead, and puts them on the top.

O Lord, the King of Glory, who, when thou hadst fulfilled all that the prophets had spoken of thee, didst, through the eternal doors, ascend to thy Father's throne, and open the kingdom of heaven to all believers; grant that while thou dost reign in heaven, I may not be bowed down to the things of earth, but that my heart may there be lifted up whither thou, our Redemption, art gone before; who, with the Father and the Holy Ghost, livest and reignest, ever one God, world without end.

Humility

Two men went up into the temple to pray; the one a Pharisee, and the other a publican. The Pharisee stood and prayed thus with himself, God, I thank thee, that I am not as the rest of men. . . . But the publican, standing afar off, would not lift up so much as his eyes unto heaven, but smote his breast, saying, God, be merciful to me a sinner. I say unto you, This man went down to his house justified rather than the other: for every one that exalteth himself shall be humbled; but he that humbleth himself shall be exalted.

Science seems to me to teach in the highest and strongest manner the great truth which is embodied in the Christian conception of entire surrender to the will of God. Sit down before the facts as a little child, follow humbly wherever nature leads, or you shall learn nothing.

Humility is the sense of our inability even with our best intelligence and effort to command events; a sense of our dependence upon forces that go their way without our wish or plan. There is a conceit of carrying the load of the universe from which religion liberates us.

The *central* sin, for the Christian, is pride and self-sufficiency. The Christian attitude has its roots in the feeling of creatureliness—the sense, not of littleness in the midst of a huge world machine or world process, but of weakness and poverty as measured by perfect Spirit.

By humility I understand such a spirit or gracious property in the soul of man as that hereby he does sensibly and affectionately attribute all that he has or can do to God, the Author and Giver of every good and perfect gift.

When I consider thy heavens, what is man, that thou art mindful of him, and the son of man, that thou visitest him? Behold, I have taken upon me to speak unto the Lord, which am but dust and ashes. Woe is me! for I am undone; because I am a man of unclean lips, and dwell in the midst of a people of unclean lips: for mine eyes have seen the King, the Lord of hosts. O God, who resisteth the proud and giveth grace to the humble, let thy everlasting mercy be continually my refuge and my confidence.

The Family

From the beginning of the creation, male and female made he them. For this cause shall a man leave his father and mother, and shall cleave to his wife. . . . What therefore God hath joined together, let not man put asunder.

If ye then, being evil, know how to give good gifts unto your children.—He called to him a little child, and set him in the midst of them.—Whosoever shall do the will of God, the same is my brother, and sister, and mother.

Jesus' teaching is full of tender allusions to parents and children, and to the natural affections which are cultivated in the home. By thus associating the family with his central religious ideas he gave it a new consecration. From the time of the primitive Church onward the Christian family has been one of the glories of our religion, and may justly be regarded as the creation of Jesus.

Jesus at the same time clearly perceived that loyalty to the family is wont to conflict with larger loyalties, and did not hesitate to affirm that in such cases it must yield. He did not thereby weaken the natural pieties. He rather exalted them and filled them with a new meaning, since they were now made to minister to the great spiritual ends of life.

It was the conviction of Jesus, and it is a great part of the distinctive message of Christianity, that the highest of our human values are the values found and developed in the life of the family.

> A home is a treasury of God
> Wherein purity, beauty and joy
> Are stored, for his purposes, inviolate.
> For a home is in itself the triumph of God,
> Banishing Night and Chaos and Necessity,
> Indwelling this lifeless clay
> With the spirit divine of freedom and joy.

O Lord, who by thy life and teaching didst consecrate the home, help us to apprehend more and more deeply the divine meaning of the family, and so to learn in and through the home the lessons of sympathy and understanding, of mutual dependence and mutual accommodation, that the spirit of the family may more and more permeate and sweeten all the relations of men with one another.

Childlikeness

Suffer the little children to come unto me; forbid them not:
for of such is the kingdom of God. Verily I say unto you,
Whosoever shall not receive the kingdom of God as a little child,
he shall in no wise enter therein.

There arose a reasoning among them, which of them should
be greatest. But when Jesus saw the reasoning of their heart,
he took a little child, and set him by his side, and said unto
them, Whosoever shall receive this little child in my name
receiveth me.—I thank thee, O Father, Lord of heaven and
earth, that thou didst hide these things from the wise and understanding, and didst reveal them unto babes.—Did ye never read,
Out of the mouths of babes and sucklings thou hast perfected
praise ?

There were, for Jesus, three stages in the life of man : the
unconscious life of the child, the conscious life of the man, and
the new life of the member of the Kingdom. In the unconscious life of the child there was spontaneity and wholeness; in
the conscious life of the man there was inhibition and division;
in the new life of the member of the Kingdom there was spontaneity and wholeness once more.

Not the pedant nor the sophist, but he alone who, with the
man's courage and the man's intellect, retains the child's heart
and the child's direct simplicity, has the necessary equipment
for understanding God's parental love towards man. Would
Christ have told others that to enter the Kingdom of heaven
they must become as little children, unless he had verified the
fact by personal experience ?

Only the assurance that the measure of the practicable is
never past experience, but is always God's call, can redeem us
from the anxieties of the worldly-wise to a fearless life of fellowship with Christ in ever fresh adventures of faith.

O thou God and Father of us all, who through Jesus Christ
our Lord didst say to those desiring to enter thy Kingdom,
" Except ye be converted, and become as little children, ye
cannot enter therein," grant us the childlike spirit. As we face
the unknown happenings of this new day, may it be with eyes
open to see what our Father would teach us, and wills resolute
to follow wherever he shall lead.

The Last First

Then answered Peter and said unto him, Lo, we have left all, and followed thee ; what then shall we have ? And Jesus said unto them, . . . Many shall be last that are first; and first that are last.

Ye know that they which are accounted to rule over the Gentiles lord it over them; and their great ones exercise authority over them. But it is not so among you : but whosoever would become great among you, shall be your minister : and whosoever would be first among you, shall be servant of all. For verily the Son of man came not to be ministered unto, but to minister, and to give his life a ransom for many.

For the kingdom of heaven is like unto a man that is a householder, which went out early in the morning to hire labourers into his vineyard. . . . And when they came that were hired about the eleventh hour, they received every man a penny. And when the first came, they supposed that they would receive more ; and they likewise received every man a penny. And when they received it, they murmured against the householder, saying, These last have spent but one hour, and thou hast made them equal unto us, which have borne the burden of the day and the scorching heat. But he answered and said to one of them, . . . Is it not lawful for me to do what I will with mine own ? or is thine eye evil, because I am good ? So the last shall be first, and the first last.

With an extreme of paradox, yet not strained one hairbreadth beyond his true meaning, Jesus strove completely to banish from the minds of his disciples the idea of justice as a law of the kingdom. The parable is one of the profoundest of all the parables ; its pure transparency opens on to illimitable depths of meaning, and the true import of the frequent phrase, " The last shall be first, and the first last," can be grasped only by its means. In the kingdom as Jesus knew it, though there is neither first nor last, yet the last are first. It is a paradox and a contradiction ; but it is the truth. For it is a kingdom of love. It could not be otherwise : love imagined, love created it. In the kingdom of love, those who belong to it find their supreme felicity in yielding to the latest comers. " There is more joy in heaven," for heaven itself is but the blessed company of the sons of God.

> Alone, O Love ineffable !
> Thy saving name is given ;
> To turn aside from thee is hell,
> To walk with thee is heaven !

To Save the Lost

The Son of man came to seek and to save that which was lost.

It is not the will of your Father which is in heaven, that one of these little ones should perish.

No recorded word of Jesus is more characteristic and more significant as an index of his own conception of his mission than the statement that he came to seek and to save that which was lost.

(David is speaking.)
Would it ever have entered my mind, the bare will, much less
   power,
To bestow on this Saul what I sang of, the marvellous dower
Of the life he was gifted and filled with? to make such a
   soul,
Such a body, and then such an earth for insphering the whole?
And doth it not enter my mind (as my warm tears attest),
These good things being given, to go on, and give one more, the
   best?
Ay, to save and redeem and restore him, maintain at the height
This perfection. . . .
Interpose at the difficult minute, snatch Saul the mistake,
Saul the failure, the ruin he seems now—and bid him awake
From the dream, the probation, the prelude, to find himself set
Clear and safe in new light and new life. . . .
Would I suffer for him that I love?   So wouldst thou—so wilt
   thou!
So shall crown thee the topmost, ineffablest, uttermost crown—
And thy love fill infinitude wholly, nor leave up nor down
One spot for the creature to stand in!   It is by no breath,
Turn of eye, wave of hand, that salvation joins issue with
   death!

Enlarge our souls with a divine charity, that we may hope all things, endure all things; and become messengers of thy healing mercy to the grievances and infirmities of men.

Immortality

He is not the God of the dead, but of the living : for all live unto him.

Whether we live, we live unto the Lord; or whether we die, we are the Lord's.—I know him whom I have believed, and I am persuaded that he is able to guard that which I have committed unto him.—Father, into thy hands I commend my spirit.—I am persuaded, that neither death, nor life . . . shall be able to separate us from the love of God, which is in Christ Jesus our Lord.

The faith of Jesus in human immortality rests upon his own experience of the character of God and the deathless nature of fellowship with him.

I must make my choice. There are things which make it hard to believe in a living, loving God. But reflection shows that it is harder still to accept the paradox that all is accident. I make my choice. What follows ? If a human parent would not allow the extinction of a cherished child, is God likely to consent to such a thing ? Will he be content to treat a living personality like a rocket which, once its cascade of stars has been displayed, has fulfilled its function and falls back unregarded into the surrounding gloom ? In the belief in immortality the rationality of the Universe is at stake.

After this it was noised abroad that Mr. Valiant-for-truth was taken with a summons. . . . When the day that he must go hence was come, many accompanied him to the river-side; into which as he went he said, " Death, where is thy sting ? " And as he went down deeper, he said, "Grave, where is thy victory ? " So he passed over, and all the trumpets sounded for him on the other side.

> For tho' from out our bourne of Time and Place
>   The flood may bear me far,
> I hope to see my Pilot face to face
>   When I have crost the bar.

Grant us the assurance that in the grasp of thy love all is utterly safe; that our souls may commit unto thee our life, and what is dearer by far than our life, with certainty, unflinching and absolute that in thy home, with thee, to thine own children, never through all eternity, can harm befall.

F

The Love of God

What commandment is the first of all ?   Jesus answered . . .
Thou shalt love the Lord thy God with all thy heart, and with all
thy soul, and with all thy mind, and with all thy strength.

Once grant the existence of a personal God—the source of all
goodness, beauty and truth—love is the only expression of the
ideal attitude of man towards him.

(Brother Lawrence said) that he had long been troubled in
mind from a sure belief that he was lost, but that he had
thus reasoned with himself about it : " I engaged in a religious
life only for the love of God, and I have endeavoured to
act only for him; whatever becomes of me, whether I be lost or
saved, I will always continue to act purely for the love of God."
That since then he had passed his life in perfect liberty and continual joy.   That when an occasion of practising some virtue
offered, he addressed himself to God, saying, " Lord, I cannot
do this unless thou enablest me "; and that then he received
strength more than sufficient.   So having accustomed himself
to do everything for the love of God, and with prayer upon all
occasions for his grace to do his work well, he had found everything easy for fifteen years.

True love of God often consists in a firm, dry resolution to
give up everything for Him.

> Love thy God and love him only :
> And thy breast will ne'er be lonely.
> In that one great Spirit meet
> All things mighty, grave and sweet.
> Vainly strives the soul to mingle
> With a being of our kind :
> Vainly hearts with our hearts are twined :
> For the deepest still is single. . . .
> Mortal !   Love that Holy One !
> Or dwell for aye alone.

O God, who art worthy of a greater love than we can either
give or understand; fill our hearts with such love towards thee
that nothing may seem too hard for us to do or to suffer in
obedience to thy will; and grant that thus loving thee, we may
become daily more like unto thee, and finally obtain the crown
of life which thou hast promised to those that love thee.

Love of Neighbour

Thou shalt love thy neighbour as thyself.

All things therefore whatsoever ye would that men should do unto you, even so do ye also unto them : for this is the law and the prophets.—Owe no man anything, save to love one another : for he that loveth his neighbour hath fulfilled the law.—He that loveth his brother abideth in the light, and there is none occasion of stumbling in him.

It is in intercourse with our fellow-men that we can exercise those qualities which make us akin to God—love, pity, forgiveness, self-sacrifice. The more we spend ourselves for our neighbours the more we attain to our own true life.

There are only two duties which our Lord requires of us, namely, the love of God and the love of our neighbour. . . . In my opinion, the surest sign for discovery whether we observe these two duties is the love of our neighbour; since we cannot know whether we love God, though we may have strong proof of it; but this can be more easily discovered respecting the love of our neighbour. And be assured that the further you advance in that love the more you will advance in the love of God likewise.

It is utterly impossible to separate loving one's neighbour from its first source, in loving God; until you can love your neighbour with God's love, you cannot really love him; until you know God you cannot know what his love is. The loving of men which can exist apart from the knowing of God is not love, as Jesus meant it, at all. The man who knows God, knows immediately that he must forgive his enemies; and the man who does not know, immediately, that he must not resist evil, does not know God.

Grant unto us, O Lord God, that we may love one another unfeignedly; for where love is, there art thou; and he that loveth his brother is born of thee, and dwelleth in thee, and thou in him. Therefore, O Lord, shed thy love into our hearts, that we may love thee, and our brethren in thee and for thee, as all children to thee.

Patience

In your patience ye shall win your souls.

That in the good ground, these are such as in an honest and good heart, having heard the word, hold it fast, and bring forth fruit with patience.—As ministers of God, in much patience.—Therefore let us also, seeing we are compassed about with so great a cloud of witnesses, lay aside every weight, and the sin which doth so easily beset us, and let us run with patience the race that is set before us.—Strengthened with all power, according to the might of his glory, unto all patience and longsuffering with joy.—If we hope for that which we see not, then do we with patience wait for it.

Patience expresses the characteristic of the man who is unswerved from his deliberate purpose and loyalty by even the greatest trials and sufferings.

> For patience, sovereign o'er transmuted ill.

> But patience is more oft the exercise
> Of saints, the trial of their fortitude,
> Making them each his own deliverer
> And victor over all
> That tyrannie or fortune can inflict.

Doth God exact day-labour, light deny'd ?
I fondly ask : But Patience, to prevent
That murmur, soon replies, God doth not need
Either man's work or his own gifts : who best
Bear his mild yoke, they serve him best : his state
Is kingly : Thousands at his bidding speed,
And post o'er land and ocean without rest :
They also serve who only stand and wait.

God of our life, there are days when the burdens we carry chafe our shoulders and weigh us down; when the road seems dreary and endless, the skies grey and threatening; when our lives have no music in them, and our hearts are lonely, and our souls have lost their courage. Flood the path with light, we beseech thee ; turn our eyes to where the skies are full of promise ; tune our hearts to brave music ; give us the sense of comradeship with heroes and saints of every age ; and so quicken our spirits that we may be able to encourage the souls of all who journey with us on the road of life, to thy honour and glory.

Watchfulness

Watch therefore, for ye know not the day nor the hour.

Be ye also ready : for in an hour that ye think not the Son of man cometh.—Let your loins be girded about, and your lamps burning; and be ye yourselves like unto men looking for their lord, when he shall return from the marriage feast; that, when he cometh and knocketh, they may straightway open unto him. Blessed are those servants, whom the lord when he cometh shall find watching.

When I seek out the sources of my thoughts, I find they had their beginning in fragile chance. Slight the impulse that made me take this turning at the cross-roads, trivial and fortuitous the meeting, and light as gossamer the thread that first knit me to my friend. These are full of wonder; more mysterious are the moments that must have brushed me with their wings and passed me by; when Fate beckoned and I did not see it, when new Life trembled for a second on the threshold; but the word was not spoken, the hand was not held out, and the Might-have-been shivered and vanished, dim as a dream, into the " waste realms " of non-existence.

> With parted lips and outstretched hand
> And listening ears thy servant stands,
> Call thou early, call thou late,
> To thy great service dedicate.

O thou divine Spirit that in all events of my life art knocking at the door of my heart, help me to respond to thee. I would take them all as good and perfect gifts from thee. I would receive even the sorrows of my life as disguised gifts from thee. Whether thou comest in sunshine or in rain, I would take thee into my heart joyfully. Thou art thyself more than the sunshine; thou art thyself compensation for the rain. It is thee and not thy gifts I crave. Knock, and I shall open unto thee.

Stir up our hearts, O Lord, we beseech thee, to prepare the ways of thine only-begotten Son; so that when he cometh we may be found watching, and serve thee with a pure and ready will.

Fidelity

His lord said unto him, Well done, good and faithful servant :
thou hast been faithful over a few things, I will set thee over
many things.

He that is faithful in a very little is faithful also in much. . . .
If therefore ye have not been faithful in the unrighteous mammon, who will commit to your trust the true riches ?—It is as
when a man, sojourning in another country, having left his
house, and given authority to his servants, to each one his work,
commanded also the porter to watch.—I have fought the good
fight, I have finished the course, I have kept the faith.

Men are to think of themselves as stewards appointed by
God, to whom they owe an unlimited service. In small things
as in great they must be faithful, conscious at all times that
the highest issues may depend on their loyalty. . . . By their
fidelity in the small things God is testing men continually to
discover whether they are worthy to be received into his
Kingdom.

If this life be not a real fight, in which something is eternally
gained for the universe by success, it is no better than a game of
private theatricals from which one may withdraw at will. But
it *feels* like a real fight—as if there were something really wild
in the universe which we with all our idealities and faithfulnesses
are needed to redeem ; and first of all to redeem our own hearts
from atheisms and fears. The deepest thing in our nature is
this dumb region of the heart in which we dwell alone with our
willingnesses and unwillingnesses, our faiths and our fears. The
faithful fighters of this hour may turn to the faint-hearted, who
here decline to go on, with words like those with which Henry
IV greeted the tardy Crillon after a great battle had been
gained : " Hang yourself, brave Crillon ! we fought at Arques,
and you were not there."

Cheered by the presence of God, I will do at the moment,
without anxiety, according to the strength which he shall give
me, the work that his providence assigns me. I will leave the
rest ; it is not my affair.

Teach us, good Lord, to serve thee with loyal and steadfast
hearts ; to give and not to count the cost ; to fight and not to
heed the wounds ; to toil and not to seek for rest ; to labour and
not to ask for any reward save that of knowing that we do thy
will ; through Jesus Christ our Lord.

The Ultimate Test

When the Son of man shall come in his glory, and all the angels with him, then shall he sit on the throne of his glory : and before him shall be gathered all the nations. . . . Then shall the King say unto them on his right hand, Come, ye blessed of my Father, inherit the kingdom prepared for you from the foundation of the world : for I was an hungered, and ye gave me meat : I was thirsty, and ye gave me drink : I was a stranger, and ye took me in : naked, and ye clothed me : I was sick, and ye visited me : I was in prison, and ye came unto me. Then shall the righteous answer him, saying, Lord, when saw we thee an hungered, and fed thee ? . . . And the King shall answer and say unto them, Verily I say unto you, Inasmuch as ye did it unto one of these my brethren, even these least, ye did it unto me.

Such was the last of Jesus' parables; £tly the last : for it is the greatest of all. Into its lovely simplicity he gathered all his knowledge. He is the great Judge; but he judges men by the love they have shown, not to himself, not to his chosen, but to any man. For all men were his brothers. By their love, and by their love alone, would this Judge judge mankind. One forgotten act of love should save a man's soul alive; one cup of cold water given in love to a beggar on the highway should bring a man into the kingdom, and make him the brother of God's only Son. One act of love and we live; and the loveless ones are damned everlastingly. The gentlest, the sternest, the most inexorable judgment ever to be passed on man : for it is endorsed by the secret soul of man.

> Some may perchance, with strange surprise,
> Have blundered into Paradise.
> In vasty dusk of life abroad,
> They fondly thought to err from God,
> Nor knew the circle that they trod;
> And, wandering all the night about,
> Found them at morn where they set out.
> Death dawned; Heaven lay in prospect wide :—
> Lo ! they were standing by his side.

O God, whose nature is Love, teach us to recognize the revelation of thyself in every act of love, and in showing love to our fellow-men to enter into thy kingdom and become one with thee.

Greatness in Christ's Kingdom

I am in the midst of you as he that serveth.

Jesus knowing that his hour was come . . . , having loved his own which were in the world, he loved them unto the end. And during supper . . . Jesus, knowing that the Father had given all things into his hands, and that he came forth from God, and goeth unto God, riseth from supper, and layeth aside his garments; and he took a towel, and girded himself. Then he poureth water into the bason, and began to wash the disciples' feet, and to wipe them with the towel wherewith he was girded. . . . So when he had washed their feet, and taken his garments, and sat down again, he said unto them, Know ye what I have done to you ? Ye call me Master and Lord : and ye say well; for so I am. If I then, the Lord and the Master, have washed your feet, ye also ought to wash one another's feet.

In the typical transformations of love adopted by Christianity, the element of physical ministration is never lost. It is through the washing of feet, the tendance of the injured, the cup of cold water, that love finds its outlet. But it is likewise characteristic of Christianity that the personal ministration was never allowed to shrink to the level of purely objective and useful service. The cup of cold water is given " in the name " of something believed to be of cosmic importance.

The touching, entrancing beauty of Christianity consists, as much as in anything else, in its freedom from all fastidiousness. A soul that is fastidious is as yet only hovering round the precincts of Christianity, but it has not entered its sanctuary, where heroism is always homely, where the best always acts as stimulus towards being (in a true sense) but one of the semi-articulate, bovine, childish, repulsively second-third-fourth-rate crowd. When I told you of my choking emotion in reading that scene of Jesus, the Light of the World (that he is this is a historic fact), as the menial servant at the feet of those foolish little fishermen and tax-gatherers, what is it that moves me but just that huge life-and-love-bringing paradox, here in its fullest activity ? The heathen philosophies, one and all, failed to get beyond fastidiousness; only Christianity—a deeply *costingly* realized Christianity—got beyond it.

O Lord, who gavest unto thy disciples an example that they also should do what thou didst unto them, help us thy servants to learn this lesson and to become the ministers of all.

" Given for You "

And he took bread, and when he had given thanks, he brake it, and gave to them, saying, This is my body which is given for you.

That life which I now live in the flesh I live in faith, the faith which is in the Son of God, who loved me, and gave himself up for me.—As Christ also loved you, and gave himself up for us.— The love of Christ constraineth us.

We have been apt to think of him as a great teacher. He lived, some hold, the rounded and well-poised life. No, that was Sophocles. He is greater. Here is one who penetrates far deeper into things. He means to do, to achieve, something.

The human community, depending, as it does, upon its loyal human lovers, and wounded to the heart by its traitors . . . utters its own doctrine of atonement as this postulate—the central postulate of its highest spirituality : *No baseness or cruelty so deep or so tragic shall enter our human world, but that loyal love shall be able in due time to oppose to just that deed of treason its fitting deed of atonement.* . . . The new deed is so ingeniously devised, so concretely practical in the good it accomplishes, that, when you look down upon the human world, after the new creative deed has been done in it, you say first, " This deed was made possible by that treason "; and secondly, " The world as transformed by this creative deed is better than it would have been had all else remained the same, but had that deed of treason not been done at all."

I have always loved to think of devoted suffering as the highest, purest, perhaps the only quite pure form of action.

Everyone who kneels at the altar of God to receive the blessed food is brought inside a life of passion and enthusiasm and suffering and glory, of which the expression can only be found in a body broken, in a blood poured out.

> O King of earth ! the cross ascend :
> O'er climes and ages 'tis thy throne;
> Where'er thy fading eye may bend
> The desert blooms and is thine own.

We praise thee, we bless thee, we worship thee, we glorify thee. we give thanks to thee for thy great glory. . . . For thou only art holy; thou only art the Lord; thou only, O Christ, with the Holy Ghost, art most high in the glory of God the Father.

" Drink ye all of it "

And he took a cup, and gave thanks, and gave to them, saying,
Drink ye all of it; for this is my blood of the covenant.

The love of Christ constraineth us; because we thus judge,
that one died for all, therefore all died; and he died for all,
that they which live should no longer live unto themselves, but
unto him who for their sakes died and rose again.—Hereby
know we love, because he laid down his life for us: and we ought
to lay down our lives for the brethren.—Inasmuch as ye are
partakers of Christ's sufferings, rejoice.—That I may know
him, and the power of his resurrection, and the fellowship of his
sufferings.

Christ's whole life was a Cross and a Martyrdom, and dost
thou seek rest and joy for thyself?

What was the secret of Christianity, the new interpretation of
life by which it conquered the world? The answer is in a sense
a commonplace. It was the lesson of self-sacrifice, of life for
others, precisely through which, nevertheless, the truest and
intensest realization of the self was to be attained—in the
Pauline phrase, dying to live; in the words of Jesus, losing one's
life to find it. This conception of the meaning of life, embodied
in the figure of One who spoke of himself as being among men
as one that serveth, this was the victory which overcame the
world. And if this is the deepest insight into human life, must
we not also recognize it as the open secret of the universe?
The omnipotence of God will mean neither the tawdry trappings
of regal pomp nor the irresistible might of a physical force. It
consists in the all-compelling power of goodness and love to
enlighten the grossest darkness and to melt the hardest heart.
" We needs must love the highest when we see it." It is of the
essence of the divine prerogative to seek no other means of
triumph—as, indeed, a real triumph is possible on no other
terms.

O Christ, the true Vine and the source of life, ever giving
thyself that the world may live, who also hast taught us that
those who would follow thee must will to lose their lives for thy
sake; grant us so to receive within our souls the power of thine
eternal sacrifice that in sharing thy cup we may share thy glory
and at the last be made perfect in thy love.

The Crucifixion

There they crucified him.

We preach Christ crucified, unto Jews a stumbling-block, and unto Gentiles foolishness; but unto them that are called, both Jews and Greeks, Christ the power of God, and the wisdom of God.—I determined not to know anything among you, save Jesus Christ, and him crucified.—Far be it from me to glory, save in the cross of our Lord Jesus Christ, through which the world hath been crucified unto me, and I unto the world.

It needs always to be remembered that while Paul insists on the death of Christ, he views it as much more than an isolated fact. The Cross is to him the supreme expression of the whole mind of Christ. The death, as he regarded it, was the life in its ultimate purpose of meaning. To know Christ crucified was to enter into the inmost spirit of Jesus.

The Cross is the outcome of his deepest mind, of his prayer life. It is more like him than anything else he ever did. It has in it more of him.

In the Cross of Christ we catch, focussed in one vivid moment, the eternal quality of Creative life.

> The Very God! think, Abib; dost thou think?
> So, the All-Great were the All-Loving too—
> So, through the thunder comes a human voice
> Saying, "O heart I made, a heart beats here! . . .
> Thou hast no power nor mayst conceive of mine,
> But love I gave thee, with myself to love.
> And thou must love me who have died for thee!"

> The morning breaks, the shadows flee;
> Pure universal Love thou art;
> To me, to all, thy mercies move;
> Thy nature and thy name is Love.

> The speechless awe that dares not move,
> And all the silent Heaven of love.

Almighty God, we beseech thee graciously to behold this thy family, for which our Lord Jesus Christ was content to be betrayed, and given up into the hands of wicked men, and to suffer death upon the Cross, who now liveth and reigneth with thee and the Holy Ghost, world without end.

The Resurrection

He is risen.

Him . . . ye by the hand of lawless men did crucify and slay : whom God raised up.—Wherefore also he is able to save to the uttermost them that draw near unto God through him, seeing he ever liveth to make intercession for them.—The exceeding greatness of his power to us-ward who believe, according to that working of the strength of his mind which he wrought in Christ, when he raised him from the dead.—If then ye were raised together with Christ, seek the things that are above.

If Jesus Christ be unique in faith and hope and love, it is unreasonable to maintain that it is impossible or even improbable that he should rise from the dead. We have not fathomed the secret of the joy of the men of the first age until we see that the Resurrection was for them the prophecy of the coming death of all sorrow, that it was in very truth " an anticipation of immortality," and a fragment of heaven here in the world of time. It is the real cause of the radical optimism of Christianity. Here, in the Resurrection, a new influx from the world of Spirit comes breaking into the world of time. As some grey ruin of a vanished past towers over a hidden city, a fragment of a vanished age of war, and stands there inexplicable until in thought you recreate its past—a survival of " old, unhappy, far-off things and battles long ago "—so stands the Christian life in the world of to-day. It is inexplicable in terms of the world of time. But it is not a survival of the past ; it is a fragment of the future, of the heaven that is to be.

The disciples did not assert merely that their Master had survived death, but that he had conquered death. They saw in the Resurrection an act of God in the life of Christ which matched at every point the apparent defeat which he suffered on the Cross.

> Thou hast conquered in the fight,
> Thou hast brought us life and light.

O God, who through thine only begotten Son Jesus Christ hast overcome death and opened unto us the gate of everlasting life ; grant that, as he was raised from the dead by the glory of the Father, so we also may walk in newness of life and seek those things which are above, where with thee, O Father, and the Holy Spirit, he liveth and reigneth for ever and ever.

More Blessed to Give

Remember the words of the Lord Jesus, how he himself said,
It is more blessed to give than to receive.

Give to him that asketh thee.—Give, and it shall be given
unto you.—Freely ye received, freely give.—The Son of man
came not to be ministered unto, but to minister, and to give his
life a ransom for many.—This is my body which is given for
you.—The Son of God, who . . . gave himself up for me.

What Jesus desired was not an indolent good-nature, willing
to be imposed on by anybody, but a royal generosity. You are
to measure your benefits not by the conduct of others but by the
self-forgetting goodness that wells up in your own heart.

The essence of the moral law, in the view of Tolstoi, the
essence that makes it God's law, is simple enough; is simple
enough, in fact, to torpedo the whole Western system of
morality. It is just " give more than you get "—always. But
Western morality says that the only principle by which human
nature can be got to move is " get, whenever possible, more
than you give." Tolstoi's achievement is to have brought all
the teaching of the Eastern prophets and saints into one formula,
the most revolutionary that was ever devised.

> Rejoice we are allied
> To That which doth provide
> And not partake, effect and not receive !
>
> For Mercy, Courage, Kindness, Mirth,
> There is no measure upon earth.
> Nay, they wither, root and stem,
> If an end be set to them.
> Overbrim and overflow,
> If your own heart you would know;
> For the spirit born to bless
> Lives but in its own excess.

O God, who in thy Son Jesus Christ has shown to us the true
meaning of life, grant that we may be converted and renewed in
our minds, so that we may know that only in giving and spending
ourselves do we truly live.

The Habit of Prayer

Pray without ceasing.

Continuing stedfastly in prayer.—With all prayer and supplication praying at all seasons in the Spirit.

To pray without ceasing means that the constant bent and drift of the soul is towards God. The note of prayer becomes the habit of the heart, in such a way that, when we are released from the grasp of our occupations, the soul rebounds to its true bent, quest, and even pressure upon God. Every man's life is in some sense a continual state of prayer. For what is his life's prayer but its ruling passion?

Both the test and expression of the quality of a personality are to be seen in its dominant desires. No desire is ever quite the same after it has been offered up before God in prayer; a desire which has found expression in prayer is inevitably purified and elevated. Prayer, therefore, is the training-ground for character.

He who sends oftenest out these ships of desire, who makes the most voyages to that land of spices and pearls, shall be sure to improve his stock most, and have most of heaven upon earth.

> More things are wrought by prayer
> Than this world dreams of. Wherefore let thy voice
> Rise like a fountain for me night and day.
> For what are men better than sheep or goats
> That nourish a blind life within the brain,
> If, knowing God, they lift not hands of prayer
> Both for themselves and those who call them friend?
> For so the whole round earth is every way
> Bound by gold chains about the feet of God.

> Thrice blest whose lives are faithful prayers,
> Whose loves in higher loves endure.

No prayer is effectual except in so far as it is the expression of the offering of the whole life.

Grant to us, O Lord, to live in such continual communion with thee, that thou mayest become more real than everything earthly, and that thy Truth, thy Goodness and thy Beauty may more and more manifest themselves in our lives.

The Knowledge of God

If any man thinketh that he knoweth anything, he knoweth not yet as he ought to know; but if any man loveth God, the same is known of him.

Now that ye have come to know God, or rather to be known of God.—Every one that loveth is begotten of God, and knoweth God. He that loveth not knoweth not God; for God is love.—I thank thee, O Father, Lord of heaven and earth, that thou didst hide these things from the wise and understanding, and didst reveal them unto babes.

God, our own souls, all the supreme realities and truths, supremely deserving and claiming our assent and practice, are both *incomprehensible* and *indefinitely apprehensible*, and the constant vivid realization of these two qualities is of primary and equal importance for us.

That hungering and thirsting, that seeking which is ever in some real degree a finding, a being found by, God.

Truly indeed I see not that light, which is too bright for me; and yet whatever I see, I see by means of it, even as what the weak eye sees, it sees by means of the sun, though into the sun itself it may not look.

There is an inward beauty, life and loveliness in Divine truth which cannot be known but then, when it is digested into life and practice. Divine truth is better understood as it unfolds itself in the purity of men's hearts and lives, than in all those subtle niceties into which curious wits may lay it forth.

> O world invisible, we view thee,
>   O world intangible, we touch thee,
> O world unknowable, we know thee,
>   Inapprehensible, we clutch thee.
>
> Not where the wheeling systems darken,
>   And our benumbed conceiving soars !—
> The drift of pinions, would we hearken,
>   Beats at our own clay-shuttered doors.

O God, teach us to see thee in all that is; make us childlike and simple, dutiful and loyal, that in being true to the highest values we know we may increasingly apprehend thee, and know that we have been apprehended by thee.

God in Everything

Whatsoever ye do, do all to the glory of God.

I have learned, in whatsoever state I am, therein to be content.—To them that love God all things work together for good, even to them that are called according to his purpose.—Inasmuch as ye did it unto one of these my brethren, even these least, ye did it unto me.—And they brought unto him little children, that he should touch them.—Jesus therefore, being wearied with his journey, sat as he was by the well. . . . There cometh a woman of Samaria to draw water.

Everything we do, if we learn to do it simply for God, is, here and now, the one means of growing in love for him. To-day it is cooking and scrubbing; to-morrow it may be utterly different. Let us practise a genial concentration upon just the one thing picked out for us by God. More than half our life goes in wishing for things other than those sent us. Yet it is these things, as sent, and when willed and at last loved as sent, that train us for Home, that can form a spiritual Home for us even here and now.

> All may of thee partake;
> Nothing can be so mean,
> Which with his tincture " For thy sake,"
> Will not grow bright and clean.

> A servant with this clause
> Makes drudgery divine;
> Who sweeps a room as for thy laws,
> Makes that and the action fine.

> This is the famous stone
> That turneth all to gold;
> For that which God doth touch and own
> Cannot for less be told.

To those round about us there happen incessant and countless adventures, whereof every one, it would seem, contains a germ of heroism; but the adventure passes away, and heroic deed there is none. But when Jesus Christ met the Samaritan woman, met a few children, an adulterous woman, then did humanity rise three times in succession to the level of God.

Open our eyes, we beseech thee, to the glory and beauty of humble things; teach us to find in every experience of life the revelation of thy good will for us; and let all tasks that are given to us be transformed by being done out of pure love to thee.

The Greatest Thing in the World

Now abideth faith, hope, love, these three; and the greatest of these is love.

Love never faileth : but whether there be prophecies, they shall be done away, whether there be tongues, they shall cease; whether there be knowledge, it shall be done away. For we know in part, and we prophesy in part : but when that which is perfect is come, that which is in part shall be done away.

She grasps not at her rights, refuses to take offence, has no memory for injuries. . . . All tolerance is she, all trustfulness, all hope, all strong endurance.

The soul is capable of an infinite expansion, which is guaranteed and reached through love. Our destiny is to grow through love into the life of all things.

Love is the sublimest conception attainable by man; a life inspired by it is the most perfect form of goodness we can conceive; therefore love is, at the same moment, man's moral ideal, and the very essence of Godhead. A life actuated by love is divine, whatever other limitations it may have.

> For life, with all it yields of joy and woe,
> And hope and fear . . .
> Is just our chance o' the prize of learning love,
> How love might be, hath been indeed, and is.

Where did Paul learn that the greatest thing of all is love ? The new insight goes back, in the most direct way possible, to what Paul calls " the mind which was in Christ Jesus." What makes Jesus stand out from the page of history is just this : that more than anybody before or since he believed in love. And every time that either Paul or John pronounces the word " love," the remembrance of the life and death of Jesus is vividly in their minds.

O Lord, who hast taught us that all our doings without charity are nothing worth, send thy Holy Spirit and pour into our hearts that most excellent gift of charity, the very bond of peace and of all virtues, without which whosoever liveth is counted dead before thee. Grant this for thine only Son Jesus Christ's sake.

G

Creative Life

If any man is in Christ, there is a new creation.

The everlasting God, the Lord, the Creator of the ends of the earth, fainteth not, neither is weary.—God, who quickeneth the dead, and calleth the things that are not, as though they were.—Seeing it is God that said, Light shall shine out of darkness, who shined in our hearts.—Striving according to his working, which worketh in me mightily.—The earnest expectation of the creation waiteth for the revealing of the sons of God.

All the conflicts and strifes of to-day are the breaking up of the fallow ground. They are the effort to create life. They are the messengers of the coming of the Son of man. Some new freedom, some new principle of life, some new desire to grow, has been taking root in the minds and souls of men. The urge to become more creative—to gain more of life and to give more of life—becomes at last intense.

But here is the finger of God, a flash of the will that can,
  Existent behind all laws, that made them and, lo, they are !
And I know not if, save in this, such gift be allowed to man,
  That out of three sounds he frame, not a fourth sound, but a star.

If Christ is our portrait of the Father, he is no less our portrait of the Holy Ghost. The characteristic expression of the Spirit, as seen in Christ's life, is constructive thought and creative effort. To-day everyone is crying out for the creative spirit. And this, if only we will see it, is the spirit manifested in the life of Christ.

We cannot long reflect on the life and character of Christ without perceiving that it is a perfect embodiment in concrete experience of an ideal principle—the principle of Creative Love. Not proof, but all the weight of probability, points to the conclusion that in that principle of Creative Love, which in the life and character of the Christ found for once undimmed expression, we have a glimpse of the quality inherent in Reality.

O God, the Creator of all things, who art perpetually renewing the face of the world and hast created us anew in Christ Jesus, grant that in the worship of thee and in communion with thee thy creative energy may more and more flood our lives, so that we may play our part in the fulfilment of thy purpose, which transcends all that we can think or understand.

The Covenant of the Spirit

God; who also made us sufficient as ministers of a new covenant; not of the letter, but of the spirit : for the letter killeth, but the spirit giveth life.

Christ is the end of the law unto righteousness to every one that believeth.—Ye are all sons of God through Christ Jesus.

Not only did Jesus reduce the Law to its purely ethical requirements, and simplify even these until they could all be comprised in one or two, but he showed that in the last resort the very idea of law must give place to another. The commandments were indeed binding, but they constituted a law which was imposed from without. Even if obedience were possible, it would have no moral worth. The external acts might be blameless, but they would be no test of the man himself. The real task of men was to attain to a moral autonomy. They were to bring their wills into such harmony with the will of God that on every occasion, however new and unexpected, they should know what God desired of them, and do it of their own accord. Christianity has never yet risen to the height of this ideal of Jesus. Paul, indeed, with his clear insight into the central meaning of the Gospel, declared that the Law had now been abolished and had been replaced by the living Spirit; but the Church has never found courage to follow him.

Men are so to identify themselves with the Kingdom that the higher will becomes their own, and all their moral action will then be spontaneous. No deliberate self-discipline will be necessary, for the new nature will express itself in their lives without their knowing. The purpose of Jesus, as Paul discerned, was not to enforce a rule that must be followed with labour and difficulty, but to impart a spirit which would take the place of law.

Would men understand, would even his own disciples understand, that the freedom that he claimed came solely from a knowledge of God? Freedom without that knowledge was licence and sin. To know God is to be so deeply one with him that a man's will is God's will.

O Spirit of Truth, lead us out of the bondage of fear into the glorious liberty of the sons of God, that by thy witness with our spirit we may know ourselves to be children of God and joint-heirs with Christ.

Cheerfulness

God loveth a cheerful giver.

He that sheweth mercy, (let him do it) with cheerfulness.—
Wherefore, sirs, be of good cheer : for I believe God.—Rejoicing in hope.—Rejoice in the Lord alway : again I will say, Rejoice.—As sorrowful, yet alway rejoicing.—I overflow with joy
in all our affliction.

The attitude of unhappiness is not only painful, it is mean
and ugly. What can be more base and unworthy than the
pining, puling, mumping mood, no matter by what outward ills
it may have been engendered ? What is more injurious to
others ? What less helpful as a way out of the difficulty ? It
but fastens and perpetuates the trouble which occasioned it,
and increases the total evil of the situation.

There is no duty we so much underrate as the duty of being
happy. By being happy, we sow anonymous benefits upon the
world, which remain unknown even to ourselves, or when they
are disclosed, surprise nobody so much as the benefactor.

On a certain occasion St. Francis reproved one of his com-
panions who appeared sad of face, and said to him, " Why
makest thou an outward show of sorrow and sadness for thy
offences ? Let this sadness be between thyself and God, and
pray to him that of his mercy he may spare thee, and may
restore to thy soul the gladness of his salvation ; but before me
and others, study always to have joy, for it becomes not the
servant of God to show before his brother or another sadness
or a troubled face."

> Undaunted by the clouds of fear,
>   Undazzled by a happy day,
> She made a Heaven about her here,
>   And took how much with her away.

The day returns and brings us the petty round of irritating
concerns and duties. Help us to play the man, help us to
perform them with laughter and kind faces, let cheerfulness
abound with industry. Give us to go blithely on our business
this day, bring us to our resting beds weary and content and
undishonoured, and grant us in the end the gift of sleep.

The Hour of Testing

Let us also rejoice in our tribulations : knowing that tribulation worketh patience; and patience, probation; and probation, hope.

Verily thou art a God that hidest thyself.—The darkness and the light are both alike to thee.—When thou passest through the waters, I will be with thee; and through the rivers, they shall not overflow thee.—Jesus cried with a loud voice, . . . My God, my God, why hast thou forsaken me ?

Do you want to grow in virtue, to serve God, to love Christ ? Well, you will grow in and attain to these things if you will make them a slow and sure, plodding, mountain ascent; if you are willing to have to camp for weeks or months in spiritual desolation, darkness and emptiness at different stages in your march and growth. All demand for constant light, all attempt at eliminating the cross and trial, is so much soft folly and puerile trifling.

But we will come again to this Valley of Humiliation. It is the best and most fruitful piece of ground in all those parts. Indeed it is a very fruitful soil, and doth bring forth by handfuls. This is a valley that nobody walks in, but those that love a pilgrim's life. And though Christian had the hard hap to meet here with Apollyon, and to enter with him a brisk encounter, yet I must tell you, that in former times men have met with angels here, have found pearls here, and have in this place found the words of life.

Ask the saintliest men and women of this world, whether their holy watch was continuous, and they will tell you how, in every life, there are weary flats to tread, with the heavens out of sight—no sun, no moon,—and not a tint of light upon the path below; when the only guidance is the faith of brighter hours.

In all such times of darkness there is one crucial point—to form no conclusions, to take no decisions, to change nothing during such crises. To turn gently to other things, to maintain an attitude of resignation : the crisis goes by, thus, with great fruit. It is far, far more God who must hold us, than we who must hold him. And we get trained in these darknesses into that sense of our impotence without which the very presence of God becomes a snare.

Almighty and merciful God, to whom the light and darkness are both alike, and without whom nothing befalls thy children, strengthen us to meet all the experiences of life with a steadfast and undaunted heart ; help us to go on our way bravely whether it be rough or smooth, and, when the mists hide thy face, to continue patiently till they are dispersed by the sun of thy unchanging love.

Flesh and Spirit

The mind of the flesh is death; but the mind of the Spirit is life and peace.

If ye live after the flesh, ye must die; but if by the spirit ye mortify the deeds of the body, ye shall live. For as many as are led by the Spirit of God, these are sons of God.—He that soweth unto his own flesh shall of the flesh reap corruption; but he that soweth unto the Spirit shall of the Spirit reap eternal life.

. . . the great law and fact that only through self-renunciation and suffering can the soul win its true self, its abiding joy in union with God, who has left to us human souls the choice between two things alone: the noble pangs of spiritual childbirth, of painful-joyous expansion and growth, and the shameful ache of spiritual death, of dreary contraction and decay.

Our religion begins to be our romance—our most solid, sustaining romance, only on the day on which it becomes adult and quite real, that is, only on the day on which we wake up to self and determine to fight it.

> Poor soul, the centre of my sinful earth,
> Fooled by these rebel powers that thee array,
> Why dost thou pine within and suffer dearth,
> Painting thy outward walls so costly gay?
> Why so large cost, having so short a lease,
> Dost thou upon thy fading mansion spend?
> Shall worms, inheritors of this excess,
> Eat up thy charge? is this thy body's end?
> Then, soul, live thou upon thy servant's loss,
> And let that pine to aggravate thy store;
> Buy terms divine in selling hours of dross;
> Within be fed, without be rich no more:
>   So shalt thou feed on Death, that feeds on men;
>   And Death once dead, there's no more dying then.

I grasped the book, opened it, and in silence read that paragraph on which my eyes first fell—" Not in rioting and drunkenness, not in chambering and wantonness, not in strife and envying; but put ye on the Lord Jesus Christ, and make not provision for the flesh, to fulfil the lusts thereof." No further would I read, nor did I need; for instantly, as the sentence ended—by a light, as it were, of serenity infused into my heart—all the gloom of doubt vanished away.

O God, who in thy Son Jesus Christ hast made us heirs of eternal life, make us worthy of our calling, that we may not fulfil the lusts of the flesh but have the mind of the Spirit, which is life and peace.

The Will of God

Be ye transformed by the renewing of your mind, that ye may prove what is the good and acceptable and perfect will of God.

The world passeth away . . . : but he that doeth the will of God abideth for ever.—The God of peace . . . make you perfect in every good thing to do his will.

Since the very being of God is absolute goodness, we can only attain to him when we act in our narrow sphere as he does in his universe. By doing God's will in the common tasks and duties we have fellowship with God, and there is no other way.

To do the will of God meant for Jesus something very different from what is generally understood by the words. For Jesus, the will of the reborn man was *identical* with the will of God. There was no effort; it was no question of keeping commandments. The member of the kingdom did the will of God because he embodied the will of God.

> My will is not my own
>   Till thou hast made it thine;
> If it would reach a monarch's throne
>   It must its crown resign;
> It only stands unbent
>   Amid the clashing strife
> When on thy bosom it has leant
>   And found in thee its life.

Our part is to give ourselves over to God and leave ourselves utterly in his hands, being wholly his. And if ye cannot be as entirely his as ye fain would be, be his as much as ye may attain unto; but whatever ye are, be that truly and entirely; and what ye cannot be, that be contented not to be, in a sincere spirit of resignation, for God's sake and in him. So shall you peradventure possess more of God in lacking than in having.

Fill us this day with the simplicity of a divine purpose, that we may be inwardly at one with thy holy will, and lifted above vain wishes of our own. Set free from every detaining desire or reluctance, may we heartily surrender all our powers to the work which thou hast given us to do; rejoicing in any toil, and fainting under no hardness that may befall us as good soldiers of Jesus Christ; and counting it as our crown of blessing if we may join the company of the faithful who have kept thy Name and witnessed to thy Kingdom in every age.

The Peace of God

The peace of God, which passeth all understanding, shall guard your hearts and your thoughts in Christ Jesus.

Thou shalt hide them privily by thine own Presence from the provoking of all men; thou shalt keep them secretly in thy tabernacle from the strife of tongues.

There is a state of mind, known to religious men, but to no others, in which the will to assert ourselves and hold our own has been displaced by a willingness to close our mouths and be as nothing in the floods and waterspouts of God. In this state of mind what we most dreaded has become the habitation of our safety, and the hour of our moral death has turned into our spiritual birthday. The time for tension in our soul is over, and that of happy relaxation, of an eternal present, with no discordant future to be anxious about, has arrived. Fear is not held in abeyance as it is by mere morality, it is positively expunged and wasted away. If religion is to mean anything definite for us, it ought to mean nothing short of this new reach of freedom, with the struggle over, the keynote of the universe sounding in our ears, and everlasting possession spread before our eyes.

We realize at the Front that the issues of life and death are not in our hands. But just because we do the only right thing and realize that everything else is out of our power, there comes to us a peace of mind and content. We take the *one step* and trust the rest. It is the beginning of the peace of God.

There is no rest for the heart of man save in God, who made him for himself. But how shall we rest in God? By giving ourselves wholly to him. If you give yourself by halves, you cannot find full rest—there will ever be a lurking disquiet in that half which is withheld; and for this reason it is that so few Christians attain to a full, steadfast, unchanging peace— they do not seek rest in God only, or give themselves up to him without reserve. A countless host of God's faithful servants have drunk deeply of it amid the daily burden of a weary life— dull, commonplace, painful, or desolate. All that God has been to them, he is ready to be to you; he only asks that you should seek no other rest save in him.

O God, from whom all holy desires, all good counsels, and all just works do proceed, give unto thy servants that peace which the world cannot give; that both our hearts may be set to obey thy commandments, and also that by thee we being defended from the fear of our enemies may pass our time in rest and quietness; through the merits of Jesus Christ our Saviour.

Grace

By grace have ye been saved through faith; and that not of yourselves : it is the gift of God : not of works, that no man should glory.

Not by works done in righteousness, which we did ourselves, but according to his mercy he saved us.—Being justified freely by his grace.—We have this treasure in earthen vessels, that the exceeding greatness of the power may be of God.—That we should not trust in ourselves, but in God which raiseth the dead.—If we are faithless, he abideth faithful; for he cannot deny himself.

The Cross in the eyes of Paul stood for a supreme act of grace on the part of God. It followed that the cross was the revelation of the true character of God. He had hitherto been conceived as a taskmaster, rewarding men strictly according to what they could earn in his exacting service. But this, it was now apparent, was to misunderstand the nature of God. He does not bargain and pay, but freely gives. He is the God of grace, and in Christ we have the assurance of this boundless generosity of God.

The fact remains, that the more I come to take large and coherent views of my life and of its meaning, the more will the fact that, by my own traitorous deed, I have banished myself to the hell of the irrevocable, appear to me both a vast and a grave fact in my world. If any new deed can assign to just that one traitorous deed of mine any essentially novel and reconciling meaning, that new deed will in any case certainly *not* be mine.

Hard work always makes me feel both crushed in my own eyes, with the keen sense of all one's old limits, miseries and helplessnesses, *and*, nevertheless, the glorious Greatness and Love, the everlasting arms, that are at the bottom of life, at the bottom even of our own little lives.

> Think on thy pity and thy love unswerving,
> Not my deserving.

O God, whose nature and property is ever to have mercy and to forgive, receive our humble petitions; and though we be tied and bound with the chain of our sins, yet let the pitifulness of thy great mercy loose us; for the honour of Jesus Christ, our Mediator and Advocate.

Kindness

Be ye kind one to another.

Do good, and lend, never despairing; and your reward shall be great, and ye shall be sons of the Most High : for he is kind toward the unthankful and evil.—Love suffereth long, and is kind.—Put on therefore, as God's elect . . . a heart of compassion, kindness.—When the kindness of God our Saviour, and his love toward man, appeared.

> That best portion of a good man's life,
> His little, nameless, unremembered acts
> Of kindness and of love.

> To do him any wrong was to beget
> A kindness from him, for his heart was rich.

> Of the beauty of kindness I speak,
>   Of a smile, of a charm
> On the face it is a pleasure to meet,
>   That gives no alarm !

> Of the soul that absorbeth itself
>   In discovering good,
> Of that power which outlasts health,
>   As the spell of a wood

> Outlasts the sad fall of the leaves,
>   And in winter is fine,
> And from snow and from frost receives
>   A garment divine.

> Ring in the valiant man and free,
>   The larger heart, the kindlier hand ;
>   Ring out the darkness of the land,
> Ring in the Christ that is to be.

O thou God of love, who makest thy sun to rise on the evil and on the good, and sendest rain on the just and the unjust, grant that we may become more and more thy true children, by receiving into our souls more of thine own spirit of ungrudging and unwearying kindness, through Jesus Christ our Lord.

Duty

As servants of Christ, doing the will of God from the heart.

Here, moreover, it is required in stewards, that a man be found faithful.—If therefore ye have not been faithful in the unrighteous mammon, who will commit to your trust the true riches ?—I hold not my life of any account, as dear unto myself, so that I may accomplish my course, and the ministry which I received from the Lord Jesus.

The unity of the *Faerie Queene* is based on manliness. . . . It is the quality which seizes on the paramount idea of duty, as something which leaves a man no choice ; which despises and breaks through the inferior considerations and motives—trouble, uncertainty, doubt, curiosity—which hang about and impede duty ; which is impatient with the idleness and child-ishness of a life of mere amusement, or mere looking on, of continued and self-satisfied levity, of vacillation, of clever and ingenious trifling.

If we could be said to have any philosophy of life at all—and that would have been the last thing we would have thought of calling it—it would all have been comprehended in the one brief rule of " doing the right thing " ! It was with us from the very start, and our life in the army was both based and built on it.

Let us have faith that right makes might ; and in that faith let us to the end dare to do our duty as we understand it.

The primal duties shine aloft—like stars.

> I slept, and dreamed that life was Beauty ;
> I woke, and found that life was Duty.
> Was thy dream then a shadowy lie ?
> Toil on, poor heart, unceasingly ;
> And thou shalt find thy dream to be
> A truth and noonday light to thee.

And there's another country, I've heard of long ago—
Most dear to them that love her, most great to them that know.
We may not count her armies ; we may not see her King ;
Her fortress is a faithful heart, her pride is suffering ;
And soul by soul and silently her shining bounds increase,
And her ways are ways of gentleness and all her paths are peace.

O thou, who art ever the same, grant us so to pass through our days with faithful hearts, that we may be able in all things to please thy loving eyes.

The Good Fight

Fight the good fight of faith.

That . . . thou mayest war the good warfare.—Suffer hardship with me, as a good soldier of Jesus Christ. No soldier on service entangleth himself in the affairs of this life; that he may please him who enrolled him as a soldier.—I am already being offered, and the time of my departure is come. I have fought the good fight, I have finished the course, I have kept the faith.—Be thou faithful unto death, and I will give thee the crown of life.

It is not only in the world of moral action, in which individuals tend to go their own way and seek their own ends, that contingency is found. Contingency, casualty and accident belong also to the world of nature, which is the theatre of that action. Nature is an element, savage and dangerous, into which the human being is thrown to show what stuff he is made of—an element testing with merciless severity his powers of courage and endurance, but drawing from him thereby the utmost of which he is capable.

May I never falter the wide world through,
    But stand in the gate :
May my sword bite sharp and my steel ring true
    At the ford and the strait :
Bide not on bed nor dally with song
    When the strife goeth keen :
This be my boon from the Gods of the Strong !

May I stand in the mist and the clear and the chill,
    In the cycle of wars,
In the brown of the moss and the grey of the hill
    With my eyes to the stars !
Gift this guerdon and grant this grace
    That I bid good-e'en,
The sword in the hand and the foot to the race,
The wind in my teeth and the rain in my face !

Whom neither shape of danger can dismay,
Nor thought of tender happiness betray.

O may thy soldiers, faithful, true and bold,
Fight as the saints who nobly fought of old,
And win with them the victor's crown of gold,
        Alleluia.

Reverence

Receiving a kingdom that cannot be shaken, let us have grace, whereby we may offer service well-pleasing to God with reverence and awe : for our God is a consuming fire.

God is in heaven, and thou upon earth : therefore let thy words be few.—My heart standeth in awe of thy words.—Stand in awe, and sin not.—Who . . . having been heard for his godly fear, though he was a Son, yet learned obedience by the things which he suffered.

Our age may succeed in fashioning the eternal materials of life into some new, original masterpiece, but only on one con-dition—that the foundation on which it builds is the attitude which from the dawn of history has underlain all that is great in human life, namely, Reverence. There can be no higher religion than reverence for life, whatever may be the language in which it expresses itself in accordance with the innermost law of its own structure.

Religion is the vision of something which stands beyond, behind and within the passing flux of immediate things.

There is no criticism of any self or social system except in present view of a content beyond them. And that which is outside every finite system, " the Not of all that man can think or say," is precisely the absolute with which religion seeks and gains alliance. . . . Thus religion is fruitful through worship ; and may we not also say, it is the one fruitful thing in the world ?

" And yet," he said, " it wasn't religion. There was no religion in the hard work and sacrifice." " What is religion, then ? " I asked. " Religion is Adoration," was the reply.

> From this wave-washed mound
> Unto the furthest flood-brim look with me ;
> Then reach on with thy thought till it be drowned.
> Miles and miles distant though the grey line be,
> And though thy soul sail leagues and leagues beyond,—
> Still, leagues beyond those leagues, there is more sea.

> Let knowledge grow from more to more,
>   But more of reverence in us dwell ;
>   That mind and soul, according well,
> May make one music as before,

> But vaster. We are fools and slight ;
>   We mock thee, when we do not fear :
>   But help thy foolish ones to bear ;
> Help thy vain worlds to bear thy light. . . .

Hope

Blessed be the God and Father of our Lord Jesus Christ, who according to his great mercy begat us again unto a living hope.

Let us rejoice in hope of the glory of God.—Tribulation worketh patience; and patience, probation; and probation, hope: and hope putteth not to shame.—The God of hope fill you with all joy and peace in believing, that ye may abound in hope, in the power of the Holy Ghost.—Having therefore such a hope, we use great boldness of speech.—Christ in you, the hope of glory.—In hope of eternal life.—The hope set before us; which we have as an anchor of the soul, a hope both sure and stedfast and entering into that which is within the veil.

Hope is the name of a grace which is characteristic of the religion of the Bible. In reliance on the revealed character of God, it looks forward with confidence to the fulfilment of the Divine purpose. It is a principle of moral action, acting directly on the will. It inspires endurance and self-control, stability and firmness. It colours man's intellectual life. It fortifies the will. It forms a great part of heroic virtue. The heroes of faith in the Bible are also patterns of hope.

> Nor can it suit me to forget
> The mighty hopes that make us men.

> Who, rowing hard against the stream,
> Saw distant gates of Eden gleam,
> And did not dream it was a dream.

Still nursing the unconquerable hope.

> One who never turned his back but marched breast forward,
>   Never doubted clouds would break,
> Never dreamed, though right were worsted, wrong would triumph,
> Held we fall to rise, are baffled to fight better,
>   Sleep to wake.

O God, the Author and Fountain of hope, enable us to rely with confident expectation on thy promises, knowing that the trials and hindrances of the present time are not worthy to be compared to the glory that shall be revealed, and having our faces steadfastly set towards the light that shineth more and more to the perfect day.

The Word made Flesh

And the Word became flesh, and dwelt among us, full of grace and truth.

When the kindness of God our Saviour, and his love toward man, appeared.—God was in Christ reconciling the world unto himself.

When Jesus wished to make manifest to men the redemptive love of God, he invented the story of the Prodigal Son, and it is the most beautiful story that has ever been invented by anybody. Yet behind the story told was the character and life of the teller. In truth there is for us another story that is more wonderful still, a story stranger and more beautiful than any fiction. When Peter and Paul and John went about in their turn to prove that same redemptive love of God to the men of their own day, they were able to preach to them a better sermon and to announce to them a fuller Christianity than even the Master himself had been able to do; for instead of telling them the parable of the Prodigal Son, they could now tell them the history of the Passion of Christ.

In him " the Word is made Flesh "—the *meaning* of the Infinite is spoken out. In that life and death is reflected, as in a mirror, the face of God.

There is no doubt at all that the crowning glory of the Christian religion is that it is not mere teaching, but that in it the Word was made flesh. What is wrong with the world is not that there is too little teaching in it, but that there is too much— too many floating and insubstantial opinions that lack the backing of actual embodiment in a living example. It is an indisputable historical fact that it is more in what he was than in what he said that the significance of Jesus lies.

In the Christian view, the Eternal reveals the whole depths of his nature within time, thereby sets infinite tasks, and produces in the world of man the most stupendous movements.

Almighty God, who didst wonderfully create man in thine own image, and didst yet more wonderfully restore him; grant, we beseech thee, that as thy Son our Lord Jesus Christ was made in the likeness of men, so we may be made partakers of the divine nature, through the same thy Son.

The New Birth

Except a man be born anew, he cannot see the kingdom of God.

If any man is in Christ, he is a new creature : the old things are passed away; behold, they are become new.—He died for all, that they which live should no longer live unto themselves, but unto him who for their sakes died and rose again.—Neither is circumcision anything, nor uncircumcision, but a new creature.—Be renewed in the spirit of your mind, and put on the new man.

Which of the highest animals before the coming of the first tiny *homo sapiens* could conceive the human consciousness that was on the brink of birth ? To conceive it he needed to have it. It was, and is, exactly thus with the thought of the kingdom of God. That is nothing less than a total change in man's consciousness. " Except ye be born again "—after that birth man would be as different from man as man is different from the brute.

Christianity is not a religion of law, but of salvation : and as such it is not content merely with organizing and stimulating existing forces, but demands a wholly new world and completely regenerated men.

Before the rich man can enter the kingdom he must realize that his wealth is so comparatively unimportant that he is ready to give it all away rather than allow it to obscure his vision of God. The man of good social position must be prepared to become the servant of the poorest and meanest. The Jew must be prepared to fraternize with the Samaritan, and the Pharisee with the publican, on equal terms. All must be ready to give up friends, home, wealth, position and life itself.

> I did not think, I did not strive,
> The deep peace burnt my me alive;
> The bolted door had broken in,
> I knew that I had done with sin.
> I knew that Christ had given me birth
> To brother all the souls on earth,
> And every bird and every beast
> Should share the crumbs broke at the feast.

O God, who didst create all things, and when the world had grown old in sin, didst deign to renew it by the holy mystery of the Incarnation, pour down upon us the grace of the same Lord Jesus Christ, that being renewed thereby in the spirit of our minds, we may put off the old man with his deeds, and may put on the new man which is created after God.

Satisfaction

Whosoever drinketh of the water that I shall give him shall never thirst; but the water that I shall give him shall become in him a well of water springing up unto eternal life.

The Lord shall guide thee continually, and satisfy thy soul in dry places, . . . and thou shalt be like a watered garden, and like a spring of water, whose waters fail not.—He turneth a wilderness into a pool of water, and a dry land into water-springs.—Seek, and ye shall find : . . . for every one . . . that seeketh findeth.—I have learned, in whatsoever state I am, therein to be content. . . . In everything and in all things have I learned the secret both to be filled and to be hungry, both to abound and to be in want.

Already in this life we ought continuously to enjoy God, as a thing most fully our own in all our works. Great is the blindness and exceeding the folly of many souls that are ever seeking God; whilst, all the time, they are themselves the tabernacle of the living God.

Satisfaction and happiness are highly convincing states of mind (understanding by happiness not temperamental gaiety, but the subconscious and hence serious affirmation of life as a whole by the will as a whole). Children tend to adopt the beliefs of those whom they instinctively recognize as happy, and of no others.

Jesus saith, Let not him who seeks cease until he finds, and when he finds he shall be astonished; astonished he shall reach the kingdom, and having reached the kingdom he shall rest.

> Now of that long pursuit
> Comes on at hand the bruit;
> That voice is round me like a bursting sea : . . .
> " Whom wilt thou find to love ignoble thee
> Save Me, save only Me ?
> All which I took from thee I did but take,
> Not for thy harms,
> But just that thou mightst seek it in my arms.
> All which thy child's mistake
> Fancies as lost, I have stored for thee at home :
> Rise, clasp My hand, and come."

O Lord, who seest that all hearts are empty except thou fill them, and all desires balked except they crave after thee; give us light and grace to seek and find thee, that we may be thine and thou mayest be ours for ever.

H

Christian Freedom

If the Son shall make you free, ye shall be free indeed.

With freedom did Christ set us free : stand fast therefore, and be not entangled again in a yoke of bondage.—If ye abide in my word, then are ye truly my disciples; and ye shall know the truth, and the truth shall make you free.—The law of the Spirit of life in Christ Jesus made me free from the law of sin and of death.

When I succeed in freeing myself from the claims of those impulses which are unable to obtain the assent of what is deepest in me, I possess what is called inner or moral freedom. In other words, the secret of the exercise of power lies in myself, and self-mastery is the necessary presupposition of any true power over others. Inner freedom is the prototype of all freedom from external and alien influences. I become free in the spiritual sense not by refusing allegiance to values which others have experienced as higher, but by making them the ruling forces in my own life.

I saw young fellows all around me fretting to be free, to be their own sole, full masters. They fretted against this and that thing; against this and that person. They thought if only they could get away from these, they would indeed be free. But I myself could not feel that to be nearly enough. I wanted, *I had to* get rid of, not those outside conditions, not those other people; I had, somehow, to become free from self, from my poor, shabby, bad, all spoiling self ! There lay freedom, there lay happiness !

While he lives for the present age a man is enslaved by its conventions and prejudices, and is in no way different from other men. But when he seeks the Kingdom, making it his one desire to do the will of God, he is set free. He can start afresh, as if from childhood, and can unfold the true possibilities of his nature.

> They are slaves who fear to speak
> For the fallen and the weak;
> They are slaves who will not choose
> Hatred, scoffing and abuse,
> Rather than in silence shrink
> From the truth they needs must think;
> They are slaves who dare not be
> In the right with two or three.

O God, who hast taught us that we are most truly free when we find our wills in thine, help us to gain this liberty by continual surrender unto thee, that we may walk in the way which thou hast ordained for us, and in doing thy will may find our life.

The Truth

Jesus saith unto him, I am . . . the truth.

Grace and truth came by Jesus Christ.—Every one that is of the truth heareth my voice.

> Man with his burning soul
> Has but an hour of breath
> To build a ship of truth
> In which his soul may sail—
> Sail on the sea of death,
> For death takes toll
> Of beauty, courage, youth,
> Of all but truth.

The Great Man's sincerity is of the kind he cannot speak of, is not conscious of : nay, I suppose he is conscious rather of *insincerity*; for what man can walk accurately by the law of truth for one day ? . . . The great Fact of Existence is great to him. Fly as he will, he cannot get out of the awful presence of this Reality. Though all men should forget its truth, and walk in a vain show, he cannot.

Religion is force of belief cleansing the inward parts. For this reason the primary religious virtue is sincerity, a penetrating sincerity.

How much truth will a man's soul bear, how much truth will it *dare ?* That for me becomes more and more the real test. Error is not blindness, error is cowardice.

Truth is our only armour in all passages of life and death.

Christianity is the answer to the riddle set by life itself. It is the answer of a religion which has the quality of Vision and Power—the vision of truth and the power to overcome.

Though all the winds of doctrine were let loose to play upon the earth, so Truth be in the field, we do injuriously, by licensing and prohibiting, to misdoubt her strength. Let her and falsehood grapple : who ever knew Truth put to the worse in a free and open encounter ?

O God, who by the adoption of grace hast willed us to become children of light, grant, we beseech thee, that we may not walk in the darkness of error, but may ever remain openly in the splendour of the truth.

The Divine Presence

If a man love me, he will keep my word: and my Father will love him, and we will come unto him, and make our abode with him.

They shall call his name Immanuel; which is, being interpreted, God with us.—Where two or three are gathered together in my name, there am I in the midst of them.—Lo, I am with you alway, even unto the end of the world.—I will pray the Father, and he shall give you another Comforter, that he may be with you for ever: . . . ye know him; for he abideth with you, and shall be in you.

> When I have learnt to think thy radiant thoughts,
> To live the truth beyond the power to know it,
> To bear my light as thou thy heavy cross,
> Nor ever feel a martyr for thy sake,
> But an unprofitable servant still, . . .
> When I have lost myself in other men,
> And found myself in thee—the Father then
> Will come with thee, and will abide with me.

When our hearts are cold and dead, . . .
Sluggish, indifferent, uninspired—
Then of a sudden, O thou Joy of our lives,
Thou comest thyself, beautiful, strong and divine,
To stir us to gallant effort,
To condemn, by thy stern self-giving, our own self-pampering, . . .
To make life terrible and glorious,
Full of unimaginable opportunities,
Instinct every moment with decisions and duties,
Fraught with the eternal issues of the Kingdom,
Where to-day's faithfulness or sloth
Means life or death in an infinite series of to-morrows.

> God be in my head,
>   And in my understanding;
> God be in mine eyes,
>   And in my looking;
> God be in my mouth,
>   And in my speaking;
> God be in my heart,
>   And in my thinking;
> God be at mine end,
>   And at my departing.

The Divine Prevenience

Ye did not choose me, but I chose you, and appointed you, that ye should go and bear fruit, and that your fruit should abide.

God is faithful, through whom ye were called into the fellowship of his Son Jesus Christ our Lord.—If we are faithless, he abideth faithful; for he cannot deny himself.—The gifts and the calling of God are without repentance.—God chose the foolish things of the world, that he might put to shame them that are wise; and God chose the weak things of the world, that he might put to shame the things that are strong; and the base things of the world, and the things that are despised, did God choose, yea and things that are not, that he might bring to nought the things that are : that no flesh should glory before God.—I press on, if so be that I may apprehend that for which also I was apprehended by Christ Jesus.

Do you wake ? Well, he too is awake. If you arise in the night-time, if you anticipate to your utmost your earliest awaking, you will already find him waking—you will never anticipate his own awakeness. In such an intercourse you will always be rash if you attribute any priority and predominant share to yourself; for he loves both more than you love, and before you love at all.

Religion, even more than all other convictions that claim correspondence with the real, begins and proceeds and ends with the Given—with existences, realities, which environ and penetrate us, and which we have always anew to capture and to combine, to fathom and to apprehend.

> I cannot ope mine eyes,
> But thou art ready there to catch
> My morning soul and sacrifice.

O Lord, give us the grace of thy Spirit, early to seek out, and evermore earnestly to follow the work which thou hast appointed for us to do.

The Fighter's Joy

In the world ye have tribulation : but be of good cheer; 1 have overcome the world.

Blessed are ye, when men shall hate you, . . . and cast out your name as evil, for the Son of man's sake. Rejoice in that day, and leap for joy.—They therefore departed, . . . rejoicing that they were counted worthy to suffer dishonour for the Name.—Let us also rejoice in our tribulations.—Count it all joy . . . when ye fall into manifold temptations.—I overflow with joy in all our affliction.

> But who, if he be called upon to face
> Some awful moment to which Heaven has joined
> Great issues, good or bad for human kind,
> Is happy as a Lover.

Many are the wild free joys of the world,
The joy of diving beneath great breakers :
The joy of swift galloping over a sandy plain ;
The joy of climbing up and up, across virgin snow,
To a solitary heaven-soaring peak of the Himalya :
But keener than these is the joy of this work we share now :
The grim mysterious joy of this struggle with death and despair.
To have faced together the blast of the cholera.
Each well knowing that help there is none,
If we sicken ourselves ;
That die we must swiftly, here in the waste,
Untended, undoctored, tormented, befouled.
Ah, thus to have fought, and shoulder to shoulder,
To know that together we rescued a few from the foe—
Thank God for this joy supreme.

To struggle; to look danger in the face; to live on dry bread in order to put an end to inequities that revolt us—this for a weak philosopher perhaps means self-sacrifice. But for the man filled with energy, force, vigour, and youth it is the conscious joy of life.

O Lord, who, when thine hour was come, didst go without fear among those that sought thy life, give me such boldness to confess thee before men, and such readiness to bear thy cross, that hereafter thou mayest confess me before thy Father which is in heaven, and give me to inherit an eternal crown.

The Divine Commission

As thou didst send me into the world, even so sent I them into the world.

Peace be unto you: as the Father hath sent me, even so send I you.—My meat is to do the will of him that sent me, and to accomplish his work.

It is certainly not necessary for happiness that every undertaking should succeed; it is only necessary that it should remain open to us to believe that these lives of ours should have some total historic meaning. May there be a moment when not alone the hero, the patriot, the sage, but the simple man of quiet life and plain speech may lay aside the attitude of humility, cease to admit his possible failure, and take control of the history which at that moment is enacting itself in his presence! Must there come to everyone an hour when the connection between the success of his cause in the world and the success of his own deed lies clear before him; when he knows beyond doubt that the arc of the destiny of an idea must now coincide with the swing of his own arm?

> So with the Lord: he takes and he refuses,
>   Finds him ambassadors whom men deny;
> Wise ones nor mighty from his saints he chooses,
>   No, such as John or Gideon or I.

> Ay, for this Paul, a scorn and a despising,
>   Weak as you know him, and the wretch you see,—
> Even in these eyes shall ye behold him rising,
>   Strength in infirmities and Christ in me.

If I am really on the business of the Divine King . . . then all the resources of our Father's empire of reality must needs be at my call for the legitimate requirements of my errand. That he who is on the King's business should have the right to work miracles at need is no subject for surprise or incredulity. The real marvel is elsewhere; it lies in the fact that we mortals should be actually entrusted with the King's business.

> Abandon the sole ends for which I live,
> Reject God's great commission and so die?

We do not ask that thou wilt keep us safe, but that thou wilt keep us loyal: who for us didst face death unafraid, and dost live and reign.

The Other-Worldliness of the Gospel

My kingdom is not of this world.

Be not fashioned according to this world : but be ye transformed by the renewing of your mind.—What doth it profit a man, to gain the whole world, and forfeit his life ?—We look not at the things which are seen, but at the things which are not seen : for the things which are seen are temporal ; but the things which are not seen are eternal.

The Gospel ever remains, with all possible clearness and keenness, a promise of redemption, leading us away from the world, from nature and from sin, from earthly sorrow and earthly error, on and on to God. It cannot allow the last word to be spoken in this life. The importance of that classical beginning ever consists in calling back the human heart, away from all culture and immanence, to that which lies above both.

The expectation of the last judgment and of the kingdom of God in the near future is the root of Christianity, the first and last thing in the preaching of Jesus. The centre of gravity in religion lies in the future, and moreover in a supernatural future brought to pass by God. That is the power which gave to Christianity its impulse to the world mission and to humanity a future and hope up to the present day. It is the source of superiority to this world, at once a boundless impulse to activity on the earth and a longing for eternity, in the world against the world, in time for eternity.

Not only by his teachings, but still more by his life and suffering, Jesus created a breach with the immediate world, and deprived it and all its goods of value ; he compelled men to look beyond it, and implanted in them an imperishable longing for a new world. Whoever is repelled by his indifference to all mere worldly culture can only forthwith let the whole of Christianity go, since the revelation of a new world, opposed to the temporal sphere, is inseparable from it. This attitude of Jesus tends only the more to attract to him those who perceive the inadequacy of all mere civilization, and who see in the secure establishing of a new world upon the fundamental relation of man to the Infinite and Eternal the only possible salvation of the soul.

O Almighty God, who alone canst order the unruly wills and affections of sinful men, grant unto thy people, that they may love the thing which thou commandest, and desire that which thou dost promise, that so, among the sundry and manifold changes of the world, our hearts may there be fixed, where true joys are to be found.

Life and Knowledge

The life was manifested, and we have seen, . . . and declare unto you the life, the eternal life, which was with the Father, and was manifested unto us.

Love never faileth : but whether there be . . . knowledge, it shall be done away.—He that loveth not knoweth not God.— If any man willeth to do his will, he shall know.

That a great teacher should live his teaching is an unfamiliar conception at a time when the divorce between the intellectual consciousness and the instinctive being has become extreme. For the meaning that we naturally attach to the idea that a teacher should live his teaching is that he should live *up* to his teaching.   But Jesus had overcome the divorce between knowledge and being.   He did not live up to his teaching; he lived it.   There is no sign of effort or strain in what we know of his teaching, or of his life as a teacher.

If religion be a function by which either God's cause or man's cause is to be advanced, then he who lives the life of it, however narrowly, is a better servant than he who merely knows about it, however much.

> So to the Church ye would confine
> The world-wide realm of the Divine;
> 'Twixt Life and Doctrine set a sea
> Nowise concern yourselves to BE.
> Bliss for your souls ye would receive,
> Not utterly and wholly LIVE.

However difficult it is to know what to believe, there is always something which we know beyond all doubt to be worth doing.   Everywhere in the New Testament faith is a possession, not of the sharp-witted and clear-headed, but of the true-hearted and loyal.

O Lord, we beseech thee mercifully to receive the prayers of thy people which call upon thee, and grant that they may both perceive and know what things they ought to do, and also may have grace and power faithfully to fulfil the same.

The Transiency of Earthly Things

The world passeth away, and the lust thereof.

As for man, his days are as grass; as a flower of the field, so he flourisheth. For the wind passeth over it, and it is gone; and the place thereof shall know it no more.

> Our revels now are ended : these our actors,
> As I foretold you, were all spirits, and
> Are melted into air, into thin air :
> And, like the baseless fabric of this vision,
> The cloud-capp'd towers, the gorgeous palaces,
> The solemn temples, the great globe itself,
> Yea, all which it inherit, shall dissolve ;
> And, like this insubstantial pageant faded,
> Leave not a rack behind. We are such stuff
> As dreams are made of ; and our little life
> Is rounded with a sleep.

> But the fair guerdon when we hope to find,
> And think to burst out into sudden blaze,
> Comes the blind Fury with the abhorrèd shears
> And slits the thin-spun life.

In proportion as the years both lessen and shorten I set more count upon their periods, and would fain lay my ineffectual finger upon the spoke of the great wheel. I am not content to pass away "like a weaver's shuttle." These metaphors solace me not, nor sweeten the unpalatable draught of mortality. . . . I am in love with the green earth; the face of town and country, the unspeakable rural solitudes, and the sweet security of streets.

The athletic attitude tends ever to break down, and it inevitably does break down even in the most stalwart when the organism begins to decay, or when morbid fears invade the mind. Death finally runs the robustest of us down. And whenever we feel this, such a sense of the vanity and provisionality of our voluntary career comes over us that all our *well-doing* appears the hollowest substitute for that *well-being* that our lives ought to be grounded in, but alas ! are not.

Teach us, O Lord, to know our frailty, that we may find our refuge and repose in thy eternal changelessness.

The Conservation of Values

He that doeth the will of God abideth for ever.

For this corruptible must put on incorruption, and this
mortal must put on immortality. But when . . . this mortal
shall have put on immortality, then shall come to pass the
saying that is written, Death is swallowed up in victory. O
death, where is thy victory ? O death, where is thy sting ? . . .
Thanks be to God, which giveth us the victory through our
Lord Jesus Christ.

Ah yes, we know that if this mere tent,
Our habitation on earth, be taken down,
A solid building, reared by God, we have still,
A habitation no hands fashioned ever.
   A home eternal, in the heavens. . . .
It is not that we would fain be disarrayed of the mortal body,
Nay, but rather overdraped with the immortal,
That mortality may be drowned in the sea of Life.
Yea, and he who for this very consummation hath fashioned us
     is God,
   God, who has given us his Spirit.

The essence of all religion consists not in the solution of
riddles, but in the conviction that value will be preserved.

       For love, and beauty, and delight,
       There is no death or change.

All we have willed or hoped or dreamed of good shall exist ;
   Not its semblance but itself ; no beauty, nor good, nor power
Whose voice has gone forth, but each survives for the melodist
   When eternity affirms the conception of an hour.

The high that proved too high, the heroic for earth too hard,
   The passion that left the ground to lose itself in the sky,
Are music sent up to God by the lover and the bard ;
   Enough that he heard it once ; we shall hear it by and by.

Holy is the true light, and passing wonderful, lending
radiance to them that endured in the heat of the conflict : from
CHRIST they inherit a home of unfading splendour, wherein
they rejoice with gladness evermore.

O God, the Protector of all that trust in thee, without whom
nothing is strong, nothing is holy, increase and multiply on us
thy mercy ; that thou being our Ruler and Guide, we may so
pass through things temporal that we finally lose not the things
eternal.

God is Love

God is love; and he that abideth in love abideth in God, and God abideth in him.

Every one that loveth is begotten of God, and knoweth God. He that loveth not knoweth not God; for God is love.—We love, because he first loved us.—I am persuaded, that neither death, nor life . . . shall be able to separate us from the love of God, which is in Christ Jesus our Lord.

Few philosophers have fully realized the tremendous import of a personality whose mere occurrence in history compels us to face the possibility that Love may be even one attribute among many in the Power behind the universe.

God is love. That is the one supreme piece of good news which every New Testament writer is, in his different manner, concerned to publish to the world. Of Christian history as a whole the same thing is true. What is it that lies behind, and gives unity to, all the confusing varieties of theological system, if not the joyful Christian persuasion that the heart of the Eternal has been manifested in Jesus Christ as a heart of love?

Do I find love so full in my nature, God's ultimate gift,
That I doubt his own love can compete with it ? Here, the
    parts shift ?
Here, the creature surpass the Creator,—the end, what Began ?

        Putting the question ever, " Does God love,
        And will ye hold that truth against the world ? "

        'Tis Love ! 'tis Love ! thou diedst for me !
          I hear thy whisper in my heart ;
        The morning breaks, the shadows flee ;
          Pure universal Love thou art ;
        To me, to all, thy mercies move ;
        Thy nature and thy name is Love.

O God, we have known and believed the love that thou hast for us. May we, by dwelling in love, dwell in thee, and thou in us. Teach us, O heavenly Father, the love wherewith thou hast loved us; fashion us, O blessed Lord, after thine own example of love; shed abroad, O thou Holy Spirit of Love, the love of God and man in our hearts.

The Adventure of Faith

Now faith is the assurance of things hoped for, the proving of things not seen.

The time will fail me if I tell of . . . (those) who through faith subdued kingdoms, wrought righteousness, obtained promises, . . . from weakness were made strong, waxed mighty in war.

We shall find that almost every forward step in the progress of life could be formulated as an act of faith—an act not warranted by knowledge—on the part of the pioneer who first made it. There was little, for example, in all that the wisest fish could know, to justify the belief that there was more scope for existence on the earth than in the water, or to show that persistent endeavours to live on land would issue in the transformation of his swim-bladder into lungs. . . . When we regard the development of living forms as a continuous whole, we are forced to recognize, as immanent and operative throughout it, a sort of unscientific trustfulness that seems to have been engrained in all living things.

> Who would sit down and sigh for a lost age of gold,
>   While the Lord of all ages is here ?
> True hearts will leap at the trumpet of God,
>   And those who can suffer can dare.

> He ne'er is crown'd
> With immortality who fears to follow
> Where airy voices lead.

Once again with proud hearts we make the old surrender,
    Once again with high hearts serve the age to be,
Not for us the warm life of Earth, secure and tender,
    Ours the eternal wandering and warfare of the sea.

O thou who art heroic love, keep alive in our hearts that adventurous spirit, which makes men scorn the way of safety, so that thy will be done. For so only, O Lord, shall we be worthy of those courageous souls who in every age have ventured all in obedience to thy call, and for whom the trumpets have sounded on the other side; through Jesus Christ our Lord.

Obedience

By faith Abraham, when he was called, obeyed to go out unto a place which he was to receive for an inheritance; and he went out, not knowing whither he went.

" There's no sense in going further—it's the edge of cultivation."
So they said, and I believed it—broke my land and sowed my
    crop. . . .
Till a voice, as bad as Conscience, rang interminable changes
On one everlasting Whisper day and night repeated—so :
" Something hidden.   Go and find it.   Go and look behind the
    Ranges—
Something lost behind the Ranges.   Lost and waiting for you.
    Go ! " . . .

Yes, your " Never, never country "—yes, your " edge of culti-
    vation."
And " no sense in going further "—till I crossed the range to see.
God forgive me ! No, *I* didn't. It's God's present to our nation.
Anybody might have found it but—His Whisper came to Me.

What was his name ?   I do not know his name.
I only know he heard God's voice and came,
    Brought all he had across the sea
  To live and work for God and me ;
    Felled the ungracious oak;
    Dragged from the soil
    With horrid toil
  The thrice-gnarled roots and stubborn rock. . . .
And I ?
Is there some desert or some pathless sea
Where thou, good God of angels, wilt send me ?
  Some oak for me to rend; some sod,
    Some rock for me to break;
    Some handful of his corn to take
    And scatter far afield,
    Till it, in turn, shall yield
      Its hundredfold
      Of grains of gold
  To feed the waiting children of my God ?
Show me the desert, Father, or the sea.
Is it thine enterprise ?   Great God, send me.
And though this body lie where ocean rolls,
Count me among all faithful souls.

O God, who art seeking in every age for loyal spirits ready to obey the heavenly vision, may our ears be open to thy voice, and, when thou dost call us, may we answer, Here am I; send me.

Perfection

The God of peace . . . make you perfect in every good thing to do his will, working in us that which is well-pleasing in his sight.

Ye therefore shall be perfect, as your heavenly Father is perfect.—Till we all attain . . . unto a fullgrown man, unto the measure of the stature of the fulness of Christ.—Admonishing every man and teaching every man in all wisdom, that we may present every man perfect to Christ.

The ethic of Jesus is positive in its demand. From this conception of goodness as free and spontaneous it follows that no limit can be prescribed to it. Men are to forgive not seventy times but seventy times seven. They are to do good, hoping for nothing again, because goodness is the law of their nature and cannot be restrained.

Nothing too bad to be incurable; nothing too good to be hoped for; nothing too high to be attempted; nothing so precious that we cannot afford to give it away. Yes, even that ! For there is that within the hero which is so *rich* that he can afford to give his very life away, and be none the poorer.

It is a law of this universe that the best things shall be seldomest seen in their best form. And, therefore, while in all things that we see, or do, we are to desire perfection, and strive for it, we are nevertheless not to set the meaner thing, in its narrow accomplishment, above the nobler thing, in its mighty progress; not to esteem smooth minuteness above shattered majesty; not to prefer mean victory to honourable defeat; not to lower the level of our aim, that we may the more surely enjoy the complacency of success.

O Searcher of hearts, thou knowest us better than we know ourselves, and seest the sins which our sinfulness hides from us. Yet even our own conscience beareth witness against us, that we often slumber on our appointed watch; that we walk not always lovingly with each other, and humbly with thee; and we withhold that entire sacrifice of ourselves to thy perfect will, without which we are not crucified with Christ, or sharers in his redemption. Day by day may we grow in faith, in self-denial, in charity, in heavenly-mindedness. And then, mingle us at last with the mighty host of thy redeemed for evermore.

The Divine Guidance

He leadeth me.

He guideth me in the paths of righteousness for his name's sake.—Lead me in the way everlasting.—Thou shalt guide me with thy counsel, and afterward receive me to glory.—This God is our God for ever and ever : he will be our guide even unto death.—He that hath mercy on them shall lead them, even by the springs of water shall he guide them.—The Lamb which is in the midst of the throne shall be their shepherd, and shall guide them unto fountains of waters of life.

> There's a divinity that shapes our ends,
> Rough-hew them how we will.

> To that same lot, however mean or high,
> Toward which Time leads me, and the will of Heaven.

> Keep thou my feet; I do not ask to see
> The distant scene,—one step enough for me.

> Only for these I pray,
>   Pray with assurance strong;
> Light to discover the way,
>   Power to follow it along.

> With mercy and with judgment
>   My web of time he wove,
> And aye the dews of sorrow
>   Were lustred by his love.
> I'll bless the hand that guided,
>   I'll bless the heart that planned,
> Where glory, glory dwelleth
>   In Immanuel's land.

O God, by whom the meek are guided in judgment, and light riseth up in darkness for the godly; grant us, in all our doubts and uncertainties, the grace to ask what thou wouldest have us to do; that the Spirit of wisdom may save us from all false choices, and that in thy light we may see light, and in thy straight path may not stumble.

Growth

The path of the righteous is as the shining light, that shineth more and more unto the perfect day.

Not that I have already obtained, or am already made perfect : but I press on.—Till we all attain . . . unto a full-grown man, unto the measure of the stature of the fulness of Christ.—This I pray, that your love may abound yet more and more in knowledge and all discernment.—My little children, of whom I am again in travail until Christ be formed in you.

The thinker must so far get behind his common-sense as to substitute an explicit conception of his conscious self as an imperfect and improvable tendency towards unity for the tacit assumption that his conscious self is an already completed unity.

The formation of character is a process by which our spiritual substance from being potentially moral becomes really so. It is a succession of acts by which we gradually (but always only by ever fresh acts) change our possibilities into actualities, and again use the resultants as so many possibilities for fresh acts and achievements. The difficulty of this conception is due to our habit of conceiving character as something of an already fixed dimension, as a thing and fact, rather than an act and energy. Yet the soul is not only an energizing substance; it is itself constituted by that continuous action which is throughout God's work within the soul, and the soul's work in God.

> After the sun the rain,
> After the rain the sun;
> This is the way of life,
> Till the work be done.
>
> All that we need to do,
> Be we low or high,
> Is to see that we grow
> Nearer the sky.

Strengthen us, we beseech thee, O Lord, with the Holy Ghost the Comforter, and daily increase in us thy manifold gifts of grace; the spirit of wisdom and understanding; the spirit of counsel and ghostly strength; the spirit of knowledge and true godliness; and fill us, O Lord, with the spirit of thy holy fear, now and for ever.

I

The Communion of Saints

And after these things I saw, and behold, a great multitude, which no man could number, out of every nation, and of all tribes and peoples and tongues, standing before the throne and before the Lamb, arrayed in white robes, and palms in their hands; and they cry with a great voice, saying, Salvation unto our God which sitteth on the throne, and unto the Lamb.

That ye may be strong to apprehend with all the saints what is the breadth and length and height and depth, and to know the love of Christ.

The goodly fellowship of the prophets praise thee.
The noble army of martyrs praise thee.
The holy Church throughout all the world doth acknowledge thee.

Thou wast their Rock, their Fortress, and their Might;
Thou, Lord, their Captain in the well-fought fight;
Thou, in the darkness drear, their one true Light:

O blest communion! fellowship divine!
We feebly struggle, they in glory shine;
Yet all are one in thee, for all are thine.

In the heavenly kingdom the souls of the saints are rejoicing, who followed the footsteps of Christ their Master: and since for love of him they freely poured forth their life-blood, therefore with Christ they reign for ever and ever.

To count the life of battle good,
And dear the land that gave you birth,
And dearer yet the brotherhood
That binds the brave of all the earth.

O Almighty God, who hast knit together thine elect in one communion and fellowship, in the mystical body of thy Son Christ our Lord; grant us grace so to follow thy blessed saints in all virtuous and godly living, that we may come to those unspeakable joys, which thou hast prepared for them that unfeignedly love thee.

The distinctive feature of the Diary is the provision for record of the time spent in quiet each day. I know that some of those who have expressed appreciation of the suggestions for meditation have no use for this kind of spiritual account keeping. But others, like myself, have found it an aid against self-deception. To keep a record of the time given to prayer and meditation enables one to know how far one's actual practice accords with one's accepted standards in a matter of vital importance.

The pages for record include a column for the time spent each day, and a second column in which to note the total for the month up to date. The ruling of these pages allows for the first record being kept in minutes, and the second in hours and minutes. Space is provided for two years. In addition to the pages for record there are a few blank pages at the end of the book for noting subjects for prayer.

1st

Jan.				
Feb.				
Mar.				
April				
May				
June				
July				
Aug.				
Sept.				
Oct.				
Nov.				
Dec.				

2nd

Jan.				
Feb.				
Mar.				
April				
May				
June				
July				
Aug.				
Sept.				
Oct.				
Nov.				
D.				

3rd

Jan.				
Feb.				
Mar.				
April				
May				
June				
July				
Aug.				
Sept.				
Oct.				
Nov.				
Dec.				

4th

Jan.				
Feb.				
Mar.				
April				
May				
June				
July				
Aug.				
Sept.				
Oct.				
Nov.				
Dec.				

5th

Jan.				
Feb.				
Mar.				
April				
May				
June				
July				
Aug.				
Sept.				
Oct.				
Nov.				
Dec.				

6th

Jan.				
Feb.				
Mar.				
April				
May				
June				
July				
Aug.				
Sept.				
Oct.				
Nov.				
Dec.				

7th

Jan.				
Feb.				
Mar.				
April				
May				
June				
July				
Aug.				
Sept.				
Oct.				
Nov.				
Dec.				

8th

Jan.				
Feb.				
Mar.				
April				
May				
June				
July				
Aug.				
Sept.				
Oct.				
Nov.				
Dec.				

9th

Jan.				
Feb.				
Mar.				
April				
May				
June				
July				
Aug.				
Sept.				
Oct.				
Nov.				
Dec.				

10th

Jan.				
Feb.				
Mar.				
April				
May				
June				
July				
Aug.				
Sept.				
Oct.				
Nov.				
Dec.				

11th

Jan.				
Feb.				
Mar.				
April				
May				
June				
July				
Aug.				
Sept.				
Oct.				
Nov.				
Dec.				

12th

Jan.				
Feb.				
Mar.				
April				
May				
June				
July				
Aug.				
Sept.				
Oct.				
Nov.				
Dec.				

13th

Jan.				
Feb.				
Mar.				
April				
May				
June				
July				
Aug.				
Sept.				
Oct.				
Nov.				
Dec.				

14th

Jan.				
Feb.				
Mar.				
April				
May				
June				
July				
Aug.				
Sept.				
Oct.				
Nov.				
Dec.				

15th

Jan.				
Feb.				
Mar.				
April				
May				
June				
July				
Aug.				
Sept.				
Oct.				
Nov.				
Dec.				

16th

Jan.				
Feb.				
Mar.				
April				
May				
June				
July				
Aug.				
Sept.				
Oct.				
Nov.				
Dec.				

17th

Jan.				
Feb.				
Mar.				
April				
May				
June				
July				
Aug.				
Sept.				
Oct.				
Nov.				
Dec.				

18th

Jan.				
Feb.				
Mar.				
April				
May				
June				
July				
Aug.				
Sept.				
Oct.				
Nov.				
Dec.				

19th

Jan.				
Feb.				
Mar.				
April				
May				
June				
July				
Aug.				
Sept.				
Oct.				
Nov.				
Dec.				

20th

Jan.				
Feb.				
Mar.				
April				
May				
June				
July				
Aug.				
Sept.				
Oct.				
Nov.				
Dec.				

21st

Jan.				
Feb.				
Mar.				
April				
May				
June				
July				
Aug.				
Sept.				
Oct.				
Nov.				
Dec.				

22nd

Jan.				
Feb.				
Mar.				
April				
May				
June				
July				
Aug.				
Sept.				
Oct.				
Nov.				
Dec.				

23rd

Jan.				
Feb.				
Mar.				
April				
May				
June				
July				
Aug.				
Sept.				
Oct.				
Nov.				
Dec.				

24th

Jan.				
Feb.				
Mar.				
April				
May				
June				
July				
Aug.				
Sept.				
Oct.				
Nov.				
Dec.				

25th

Jan.				
Feb.				
Mar.				
April				
May				
June				
July				
Aug.				
Sept.				
Oct.				
Nov.				
Dec.				

26th

Jan.				
Feb.				
Mar.				
April				
May				
June				
July				
Aug.				
Sept.				
Oct.				
Nov.				
Dec.				

K

27th

Jan.				
Feb.				
Mar.				
April				
May				
June				
July				
Aug.				
Sept.				
Oct.				
Nov.				
Dec.				

28th

Jan.				
Feb.				
Mar.				
April				
May				
June				
July				
Aug.				
Sept.				
Oct.				
Nov.				
Dec.				

29th

Jan.				
Feb.				
Mar.				
April				
May				
June				
July				
Aug.				
Sept.				
Oct.				
Nov.				
Dec.				

30th

Jan.				
Feb.				
Mar.				
April				
May				
June				
July				
Aug.				
Sept.				
Oct.				
Nov.				
Dec.				

Jan.				
Feb.				
Mar.				
April				
May				
June				
July				
Aug.				
Sept.				
Oct.				
Nov.				
Dec.				

Monthly Average

Jan.	
Feb.	
Mar.	
April	
May	
June	
July	
Aug.	
Sept.	
Oct.	
Nov.	
Dec.	

INDEX OF QUOTATIONS

17. Mt. 5. 4; Isa. 51. 12; 2 Cor. 7. 6; 1. 3–4.—Stephen Phillips, " Grief and God."—Blake, " Proverbs " in *Ideas of Good and Evil.*—Abbé Huvelin, quoted von Hügel, *Selected Letters,* p. 62.—Milton, " Samson Agonistes."—X.

18. Mt. 5. 5; 21. 5; 11. 29; 2 Cor. 10. 1; Tit. 3. 2; 1 Pet. 3. 4; Ps. 25. 9.—Blake, *Songs of Innocence.*—Von Hügel, *Selected Letters,* pp. 10–11 (adapted).—X.—Chaucer, *Canterbury Tales,* Prologue.—Jeremy Taylor (abbreviated).

19. Mt. 5. 6; Ps. 63. 1; 84. 2; 107. 9; 145. 19.—X.—X.—Milton, " Comus."—Lascelles Abercrombie, " The Sale of St. Thomas."—Way, *Letters of St. Paul,* Rom. 8. 26.—*Book of Common Prayer.*

20. Mt. 5. 7; 18. 33; Lu. 6. 36; Mt. 9. 13.—Scott, *Ethical Teaching of Jesus,* pp. 85–6.—Shakespeare, *Merchant of Venice,* Act IV. Sc. 1.—Burke, *Speech at Bristol.*—X.

21. Mt. 5. 8; Ps. 24. 3–4; 1 Tim. 1. 5; Jas. 1. 27.—Sorley, *Marlborough and Other Poems,* p. 66.—Buchan, *The Dancing Floor,* pp. 309–10.—Von Hügel, *Essays and Addresses* (first series), p. 285.—Milton, " Comus."—Seeley, *Ecce Homo,* Chap. XIII.—Keble, " Blest are the pure in heart."—*Gelasian Sacramentary.*

22. Mt. 5. 9; Lu. 2. 14; Mt. 10. 34; Rom. 15. 33; Eph. 6. 15.—X.—Bacon, *Advancement of Learning,* II. xxi. 5.—Tennyson.—Clifford Bax, *Songs of Praise,* 197.—Abraham Lincoln, *Second Inaugural Address.*—*Mozarabic Sacramentary.*

23. Mt. 5. 10–12.—X.—Nietzsche, *Götzendämmerung.*—*Life of Henry Suso written by Himself,* quoted Connell, *Book of Devotional Readings,* pp. 87–8.—X.—X.

24. Mt. 5. 14; 5. 16; 5. 13; Phil. 2. 15–16; 2 Cor. 6. 3–7; Gal. 5. 22–3.—X.—X.—St. Augustine, *Confessions,* I. 1.—Keats, " Endymion."—Bruce, *Commentary on St. Matthew's Gospel.*—Hoyland, *Sacrament of the Common Life,* p. 67 (adapted).

25. Mt. 5. 45; 5. 44–5; Eph. 5. 1; Rom. 8. 19.—John Smith, quoted Connell, *Book of Devotional Readings,* pp. 165–6.—Scott, *Ethical Teaching of Jesus,* pp. 39, 41 (abbreviated).—*Little Flowers of St. Francis.*—X.

26. Mt. 5. 39–41.—Hocking, *Human Nature and Its Remaking,* pp. 349–51 (abbreviated).—Milton, " Paradise Lost," Book I, line 648.—X.

27. Mt. 6. 1; 6. 6; I Cor. 4. 3–4; Mt. 10. 28; Jno. 5. 44.—Hocking, *Human Nature and its Remaking,* p. XII.—Kipling, " If," *Songs from Books.*—Wordsworth, " The Happy Warrior."—Kipling, " Land of our Birth," *Puck of Pook's Hill,* " The Children's Song."

28. Mt. 6. 9; Isa. 6. 3.—Otto, *Idea of the Holy,* pp. 85–7 (abbreviated).—Von Hügel, *Selected Letters,* p. 124.—Von Hügel, *Essays and Addresses* (second series), p. 224.—X.

29. Mt. 6. 10; 12. 50; Jno. 4. 34; Mt. 7. 21.—X.—Troeltsch, *Gesammelte Schriften,* II. 636.—Scott, *Ethical Teaching of Jesus,* pp. 39–40.—*Ibid.,* pp. 62, 65.—Madame Guyon.—X.—X.

30. Mt. 6. 11; 6. 26; Phil. 4. 19; 2 Cor. 9. 8; 12. 9; Ps. 23. 1.—Scott, *Ethical Teaching of Jesus,* p. 66.—Brother Lawrence, *Practice of the Presence of God.*—X.—X.

31. Mt. 6. 12; 9. 2; Eph. 4. 32; 1. 7.—Royce, *Problem of Christianity,* I. 253–63 (abbreviated).—Otto, *Idea of the Holy,* p. 59.—X.—Bishop Andrewes, *Private Devotions.*—Charlotte Elliott.

Second Month.

1. Mt. 6. 12; 18. 21–22; 5. 44–45; Eph. 4. 32.—Scott, *Ethical Teaching of Jesus,* pp. 87–8.—Royce, *Problem of Christianity,* I. p. 350.—X.

2. Mt. 6. 13; Tit. 2. 10; Eph. 1. 13; Lu. 19. 10; 1 Pet. 1. 9; Phil. 2. 12–13; Eph. 6. 12.—X.—Hocking, *Human Nature and Its Remaking,* p. 279.—Von Hügel, *Selected Letters,* p. 231.—Matthew Arnold, Stagirius.

3. Mt. 6. 19–21; 19. 21; Col. 3. 1.—Way, *Letters of St. Paul,* 2 Cor. 4. 18.—Scott, *Ethical Teaching of Jesus,* p. 54.—Taylor, in *Essays Catholic and Critical,* p. 69.—Von Hügel, *Selected Letters,* p. 220.—St. Augustine.

4. Mt. 6. 24.—Way, *Letters of St. Paul*, 2 Cor. 6. 14–18.—Matthew Arnold. *Lyric and Elegiac Poems*, "The Scholar Gipsy."—X.—Ward, *Psychological Principles*, p. 468.—Tersteegen, quoted *Great Souls at Prayer*, p. 226.— Charlotte Elliott.

5. Mt. 6. 34; 6. 26; 1 Pet. 5. 7; Rom. 8. 28.—Ottley in Hastings' *Encyclopædia of Religion and Ethics*, IX. p. 700.—Scott, *Ethical Teaching of Jesus*, pp. 68, 70.—Robertson, *Spiritual Pilgrimage of Jesus*, pp. 94–5.—William Bright, quoted *Great Souls at Prayer*, p. 46.

6. Mt. 6. 28–9; 10. 29; Jno. 2. 1–2.—Edwin Markham, "Revelation," in Collected Poems, 1927—Browning, "Fra Lippo Lippi."—Von Hügel, *Essays and Addresses* (second series), pp. 218–19 (adapted).—X.

7. Mt. 6. 33; 5. 20; Ps. 45. 7; 1 Jno. 2. 29.—Cairns, *Reasonableness of the Christian Faith*, pp. 51–3 (abbreviated).—Milton, "Comus."—Wordsworth, "Ode to Duty."—Adams Brown, *The Quiet Hour*, p. 18 (adapted).

8. Mt. 7. 7–8; Mk. 11. 24; Jno. 15. 7; 16. 24.-Heiler, *Das Gebet*, p. 494.—Hogg, *Redemption from this World*, pp. 230–2, 227.—Coleridge.—Bishop Andrewes, *Preces Privatæ.—Book of Common Prayer.*

9. Mt. 7. 14; Lu. 13. 24; Mt. 18. 8; 1 Cor. 9. 26; Heb. 12, 1–2.—*New Sayings of Jesus*, from Oxyrhynchus.—Spranger, *Lebensformen*, p. 350.—Browning, *The Ring and the Book*, "The Pope," lines 1185–92.—Von Hügel, *Selected Letters*, p. 275.—*Ibid.*, p. 299.—Hoyland, *Fourfold Sacrament*, p. 94.

10. Mt. 7. 21; 7. 24–25; 21, 28–31; Jno. 13. 17.—James, *Principles of Psychology*, I. p. 124.—Barbour, *Thoughts*, pp. 70–1.—Drinkwater, "A Prayer," Collected Poems.

11. Mk. 1. 41; Lu. 7. 13; Mt. 9. 36.—Milton, "Paradise Lost," Book III.—Scott, *Ethical Teaching of Jesus*, p. 84.—Glover, *Jesus of History*, pp. 56–7.— Francis Bacon.—Shelley, "A Defence of Poetry."—Blake, "William Bond."—Coleridge, "The Ancient Mariner."—X.

12. Mk. 2. 16–17.—Middleton Murry, *Life of Jesus*, p. 77.—*Ibid.*, pp. 283–4.— Masefield, *The Everlasting Mercy*, p. 66.—Von Hügel, *Selected Letters*, p.189. —X.—Charlotte Elliott.

13. Mt. 9. 29; Mk. 10. 27; Mt. 9. 2; 8. 10; 15. 28; Mk. 11. 22–23.—Streeter, *Reality*, pp. 260, 299–302 (adapted).—Hogg, *Redemption from this World*, p. 238.—X.

14. Mt. 9. 37–8; Jno. 4. 35; Mt. 9. 36.—Stevenson, *Across the Plains*, "Pulvis et Umbra."—Myers, *St. Paul*.—Matthew Arnold, "Thyrsis."—Wordsworth, "Lines composed above Tintern Abbey."—*New Sayings of Jesus*, from Oxyrhynchus.—X.

15. Mt. 10. 22; Jas. 5. 11; Heb. 6. 15; 11. 27; 2 Cor. 6. 4–5.—Way, *Letters of St. Paul*, 2 Cor. 4. 16.—Church, *Spenser* (English Men of Letters), p. 151.— Milton, Sonnet XXII.—Kipling, "If," *Songs from Books*.—Fénelon.— Thomas Aquinas, quoted *Great Souls at Prayer*, p. 42.

16. Mt. 10. 29–31; Rom. 8. 38–9; Deut. 33. 27; Ps. 103. 13.—Baillie, *Roots of Religion*, p. 181.—Jacks, *Religious Perplexities*, pp. 92–3.—James, *Varieties of Religious Experience*, p. 285.—*St. Patrick's Breastplate.*—X.

17. Mt. 10. 32; Mk. 8. 38; Ps. 40. 10; Rom. 1. 16.—Milton, "Paradise Lost," Book VI.—Milton, *Reason of Church Government*, Book II.—Hoyland, *Fourfold Sacrament*, p. 119.—Nicholas Ridley, Bishop and Martyr, quoted *Great Souls at Prayer*, p. 151.

18. Lu. 14. 33; Mt. 10. 37–8.—Trevelyan, *Garibaldi's Defence of the Roman Republic*, pp. 231–2.—Winston Churchill, *The World Crisis*, 1916–18, Part I. 195–6.—Letter of the Churches of Lyons and Vienne to the Brethren throughout Asia and Phrygia, A.D. 177.—St. Augustine, quoted *Great Souls at Prayer*, p. 278.

19. Mt. 10. 39.—Scott, *Ethical Teaching of Jesus*, p. 55.—Newman.—James, *Varieties of Religious Experience*, p. 364.—*Ibid.*, p. 364. Newbolt, *Poems : New and Old.*—X.

20. Mt. 11. 4–5; Lu. 4. 17–21; Isa. 35. 6–7; 32. 2.—X.—Blake, "The Divine Image."—Cairns, *Reasonableness of the Christian Faith*, p. 160.—Hoyland, *Fourfold Sacrament*, p. 62.

L

21. Mt. 11. 27–29.—X.—Mackintosh, *Doctrine of the Person of Jesus Christ*, p. 399.—Jean Nicholas Grou, *The Hidden Life of the Soul*, quoted Connell, *Devotional Readings*, p. 196.—Stephen Phillips, " The Poet's Prayer."—Jacob Boehme.—X.

22. Mt. 3. 14; Lu. 22. 28; 22. 15; Jno. 15. 15; 13. 1.—Glover, *Jesus of History*, p. 75.—Browning, " The Lost Leader."—Quotations from Wordsworth, " Three years she grew," and Browning, *The Ring and the Book*, Book VI.—X.

23. Mt. 12. 33; Lu. 6. 43–5.—Hocking, *Human Nature and Its Remaking*, pp. 339–43 (abbreviated).—Scott, *Ethical Teaching of Jesus*, pp. 20, 114, 118–9.—Tennyson, " In Memoriam," CXI.—Royce, *Problem of Christianity*, I. p. 345.—X.

24. Mk. 4. 2; 4. 3–8, 26–32.—Raven, *Creator Spirit*, p. 17.—*New Sayings of Jesus*, from Oxyrhynchus.—Wordsworth, " The Excursion."—Middleton Murry, *Life of Jesus*, p. 185.—X.

25. Mt. 13. 44; Mk. 2. 19; Jno. 16. 20, 24; 2 Cor. 8. 2; 1 Pet. 1. 8; Isa. 35. 10.—Stevenson, *Across the Plains*, " The Lantern Bearers."—Von Hügel, *Essays and Addresses* (second series), p. 239.—Spinoza, quoted Bridges, *The Spirit of Man*.—*The Mirror of Perfection*.—Stevenson, " The Celestial Surgeon."—Hoyland, *Fourfold Sacrament*, p. 56.

26. Mt. 13. 45–6; 11. 12; Lu. 9. 62.—Glover, *Jesus of History*, pp. 135–8. The references are to Lu. 18. 2; Mt. 25. 4; 13. 44; Lu. 11. 8; Mk. 9. 43; Lu. 17. 27; Mt. 23. 3; 21. 28; Mk. 4. 6; Mt. 6. 24.—Seeley, *Ecce Homo*, Chap. XIII.—Burke, *A Regicide Peace*, pp. 51–2.—Newman, quoted *Great Souls at Prayer*, p. 35.

27. Mk. 6. 3; Lu. 2. 7; Mt. 18. 10; Gen. 28. 16.—Francis Thompson, " In No Strange Land."—Patmore, " The Angel in the House."—Adams Brown, *The Quiet Hour*, p. 48.

28. Mk. 8. 29; Jno. 6. 68; Isa. 32. 2; Jno. 20. 28.—Keim, *Jesus of Nazara*, IV. p. 263.—Morgan, *The Nature and the Right of Religion*, p. 110.—Von Hügel, *Mystical Element in Religion*, I. p. 26.—Bernard of Clairvaux.—Te Deum Laudamus.

29. Mk. 8. 31; Isa. 53. 3, 11–12.—Middleton Murry, *Life of Jesus*, p. 163.—Burke, *A Regicide Peace*, p. 19.—Von Hügel, *Mystical Element in Religion*, I. pp. 26–7.—X.

30. Mk. 8. 34; Mt. 10. 24–5.—Schweitzer, *Civilization and Ethics*, pp. 267–9.—Schweitzer, *Quest of the Historical Jesus*.—Jacks, *Religious Perplexities*, pp. 88–9.—" Fight the good fight," J. S. B. Monsell.—Martineau, quoted *Great Souls at Prayer*, p. 139.

31. Lu. 9. 51; Mk. 4. 40; Mt. 10. 28; Mk. 8. 34; Acts 4. 13.—Scott, *Ethical Teaching of Jesus*, pp. 107–8.—Lines published anonymously in *The Spectator*.—Hoyland, *Fourfold Sacrament*, p. 100.

Third Month.

1. Lu. 10. 20.—Harnack, *What is Christianity ?* p. 66.—Hocking, *Meaning of God in Human Experience*, pp. 414, 418.—Campagnac, *Society and Solitude*, p. 224.—Von Hügel, *Essays and Addresses* (first series), p. XIII.—Von Hügel, *Selected Letters*, p. 191.—X.

2. Lu. 10. 40–2.—Von Hügel, *Essays and Addresses* (second series), p. 227.—*Ibid.*, p. 60.—Wordsworth, " Expostulation and Reply."—X.

3. Lu. 12. 2; Mt. 6. 4; 1 Jno. 1. 5–7; 1 Cor. 5. 8.—Scott, *Ethical Teaching of Jesus*, p. 105.—Eucken, *Problem of Human Life*, p. 159.—Carlyle, *Heroes and Hero-Worship*, Chap. II.—James, *Varieties of Religious Experience*, p. 324.—Hoyland, *Fourfold Sacrament*, p. 87.—Stobart, quoted *A Book of Private Prayer*, p. 113.

4. Lu. 12. 15; 12. 20–21; 9. 25; Mt. 6. 25.—X.—James, *Talks to Teachers on Psychology and Life's Ideals*, pp. 298–9.—Tolstoi, quoted James, *Varieties of Religious Experience*, p. 185.—Keats, *Letters* (ed. Colvin), XCII.—Browning, " In a Balcony."—X.

5. Lu. 12. 32; Mk. 4. 26–7; Mt. 24, 36.—Scott, *Ethical Teaching of Jesus*, pp. 48, 50.—Schweizer, *Christianity and the Religions of the World*, pp. 29–30.—X.

6. Lu. 15. 4–7; Mt. 10. 29–31; 18. 10.—Scott, *Ethical Teaching of Jesus*, pp. 38, 83 (abbreviated).—Troeltsch, *Gesammelte Schriften*, I. p. 978.—X.—X.

7. Lu. 16. 15; Mt. 21. 31; Lu.14. 11; 1 Cor. 1. 27–28.—Scott, *Ethical Teaching of Jesus*, pp. 115–16.—*Letters of William James*, II. p. 90.—*Mozarabic Sacramentary.*

8. Lu. 18. 10–14.—*Life and Letters of T. H. Huxley*, I. p. 210.—Dewey, *Human Nature and Conduct*, pp. 289, 331.—Von Hügel, *Essays and Addresses* (second series), pp. 236, 159 (adapted).—X.—X.

9. Mk. 10. 6–9; Mt. 7. 11; 18. 2; Mk. 3. 35.—Scott, *Ethical Teaching of Jesus*, pp. 95–6, 98.—Baillie, *Roots of Religion*, p. 165.—Hoyland, *Sacrament of the Common Life*, p. 53.—X.

10. Mk. 10. 14–15; Lu. 9. 46–8; Mt. 11. 25; 21. 16.—Middleton Murry, *Life of Jesus*, p. 184.—Streeter, *Reality*, p. 185.—Hogg, *Redemption from this World*, p. 239.—Adams Brown, *The Quiet Hour*, p. 17.

11. Mt. 19. 27–30; Mk. 10. 42–5; Mt. 20. 1, 9–16.—Middleton Murry, *Life of Jesus*, pp. 232–4.—Whittier, " Our Master."

12. Lu. 19. 10; Mt. 18. 14.—Bruce, *Apologetics*, p. 48.—Browning, " Saul."—Martineau, quoted *Great Souls at Prayer*, p. 356.

13. Lu. 20. 38; Rom. 14. 8; 2 Tim. 1. 12; Lu. 23. 46; Rom. 8. 38–9.—X.—Streeter, *Reality*, p. 315.—Bunyan, *Pilgrim's Progress*, Book II.—Tennyson, " Crossing the Bar."—Hoyland, *Fourfold Sacrament*, p. 95.

14. Mk. 12. 28–30.—Streeter, *Reality*, p. 207.—Brother Lawrence, *Practice of the Presence of God*.—Fénelon.—Sir Aubrey de Vere, " Reality."—X.

15. Mk. 12. 31; Mt. 7. 12; Rom. 13. 8; 1 Jno. 2. 10.—Scott, *First Age of Christianity*, pp. 101–2.—St. Teresa, *The Interior Castle*, quoted Connell, *A Book of Devotional Readings*, pp. 131–2.—Middleton Murry, *Life of Jesus*, pp. 191–2.—X.

16. Lu. 21. 19; 8. 15; 2 Cor. 6. 4; Heb. 12. 1; Col. 1. 11; Rom. 8. 25.—X.—Samuel Johnson, *Vanity of Human Wishes*.—Milton, " Samson Agonistes."—Milton, Sonnet " On his Blindness."—X.

17. Mt. 25. 13; 24. 44; Lu. 12. 35–7.—Logan Pearsall Smith, *Trivia*.—Sorley. " Expectans Expectavi," *Marlborough and Other Poems*.—Matheson, quoted *Great Souls at Prayer*, p. 101.—X.

18. Mt. 25. 21; Lu. 16. 10–11; Mk. 13. 34; 2 Tim. 4. 7.—Scott, *Ethical Teaching of Jesus*, pp. 105–6.—James, *The Will to Believe*, pp. 61–2.—Fénelon.—X.

19. Mt. 5. 31–40.—Middleton Murry, *Life of Jesus*, pp. 274–5.—Francis Thompson, *A Judgment of Heaven*, Epilogue.—X.

20. Lu. 22. 27; Jno. 13. 1–14.—Hocking, *Human Nature and Its Remaking*, pp. 367–8 (abbreviated).—Von Hügel, *Selected Letters*, p. 258 (adapted).—X.

21. Lu. 22. 29; Gal. 2. 20; Eph. 5. 2; 2 Cor. 5. 14.—Glover, *Jesus of History*, pp. 179–80.—Royce, *Problem of Christianity*. I. pp. 322, 307–8.—Von Hügel, *Selected Letters*, p. 70.—Scott Holland.—James Martineau, " A voice upon the midnight air," *Songs of Praise*, 71.—X

22. Mt. 26. 27–8; 2 Cor. 5. 14–15; 1 Jno. 3. 16; 1 Pet. 4. 13; Phil. 3. 10.—Thomas à Kempis, *Imitation of Christ*.—Pringle-Pattison, *The Idea of God*, pp. 410–11 (abbreviated).—*The Kingdom, the Power and the Glory*, p. 70.

23. Lu. 23. 33; 1 Cor. 1. 23–24; 2. 2; Gal. 6. 14.—Scott, *Fourth Gospel*, p. 20.—Glover, *Jesus of History*, p. 188.—Streeter. *Reality*, p. 232.—Browning, " An Epistle."—Charles Wesley, " Come, O Thou Traveller Unknown."—X.—*Book of Common Prayer.*

24. Mk. 16. 6; Acts 2. 23–4; Heb. 7. 25; Eph. 1. 19–20; Col. 3. 1.—Cairns in *Christ and Human Need*, pp. 178, 186–8.—Selwyn in *Essays Catholic and Critical*, p. 314 (adapted).—X.—*New Prayer Book*, p. 75.

25. Acts 20. 35; Mt. 5. 42; Lu. 6. 38; Mt. 10. 8; 20. 28; Lu. 22. 19; Gal. 2. 20.—Scott, *Ethical Teaching of Jesus*, p. 87.—Willcocks, *Between the Old World and the New*, p. 231.—Browning, " Rabbi Ben Ezra."—Lawrence Binyon, *The Secret*.—X.

26. 1 Thess. 5. 17; Rom. 12. 12; Eph. 6. 18.—Forsyth, *Power of Prayer*, pp. 64–5 (abbreviated).—Streeter, *Reality*, p. 291.—Archbishop Leighton on 1 Pet. 4. 7.—Tennyson, *Idylls of the King*, "Passing of Arthur."—Tennyson, "In Memoriam," XXXII.—X.—X.

27. 1 Cor. 8. 2–3; Gal. 4. 9; 1 Jno. 4. 7–8; Mt. 11. 25.—Von Hügel, *Selected Letters*, p. 71.—*Ibid.*, p. 191.—St. Anselm.—John Smith, quoted Connell, *Book of Devotional Readings*, p. 163.—Francis Thompson, "In No Strange Land."—X.

28. 1 Cor. 10. 31; Phil. 4. 11; Rom. 8. 28; Mt. 25, 40; Mk. 10. 13; Jno. 4. 6–7.—Von Hügel, *Selected Letters*, p. 306.—George Herbert, "Teach me, my God and King."—Maeterlinck, *Wisdom and Destiny.*—X.

29. 1 Cor. 13. 13. 13. 8–10.—Way, *Letters of St. Paul*, 1 Cor. 13. 5–7.—Fotheringham, *Studies of the Mind and Art of Robert Browning*, p. 230.—Jones, *Browning as a Philosophical and Religious Teacher*, p. 143.—Browning, "A Death in the Desert."—Baillie, *Roots of Religion*, p. 159.—*Book of Common Prayer.*

30. 2 Cor. 5. 17 (marg.); Isa. 40. 28; Rom. 4. 17; 2 Cor. 4. 6; Col. 1. 29; Rom. 8. 19.—*Sanderson of Oundle*, pp. 213–4.—Browning, "Abt Vogler."—Streeter, *The Spirit*, p. 371 (abbreviated).—Streeter, *Reality*, pp. 209, 213.—X.

31. 2 Cor. 3. 6; Rom. 10. 4; Gal. 3. 26.—Scott, *Ethical Teaching of Jesus*, pp. 35–6 (adapted).—*Ibid.*, pp. 118, 119.—Middleton Murry, *Life of Jesus*, p. 82 (abbreviated).—X.

Fourth Month.

1. 2 Cor. 9. 7; Rom. 12. 8; Acts 27. 25; Rom. 12. 12; Phil. 4. 4; 2 Cor. 6. 10; 7. 4.—James, *Varieties of Religious Experience*, p. 89.—Stevenson, "An Apology for Idlers" in *Virginibus Puerisque.*—*The Mirror of Perfection.*—Houghton, "In Memoriam."—Stevenson, *Vailima Papers.*

2. Rom. 5. 3–4; Isa. 45. 15; Ps. 139. 12; Isa. 42. 2; Mk. 15. 34.—Von Hügel, *Selected Letters*, p. 266 (abbreviated).—Bunyan, *Pilgrim's Progress* (abbreviated).—Martineau, *Hours of Thought.*—Von Hügel, *Selected Letters*, p. 305 (abbreviated).—X.

3. Rom. 8. 6; 13–4; Gal. 6. 8.—Von Hügel, *The Mystical Element in Religion*, II. p. 395.—Von Hügel, *Selected Letters*, p. 352.—Shakespeare, *Sonnets.*—St. Augustine, Confessions.—X.

4. Rom. 12. 2; 1 Jno. 2. 17; Heb. 13. 20–21.—Scott, *The First Age of Christianity*, pp. 97–8.—Middleton Murry, *Life of Jesus*, p. 185.—Matheson, "Make me a captive, Lord."—John Tauler, quoted Connell, *Book of Devotional Readings*, p. 91.—Martineau, quoted *Great Souls at Prayer*, p. 39.

5. Phil. 4. 7; Ps. 31. 23 (Prayer Book).—James, *Varieties of Religious Experience*, pp. 47–8.—Young, *A Soldier to the Church*, p. 133.—Jean Nicholas Grou, quoted Connell, *Book of Devotional Readings*, p. 196 (abbreviated).—X.

6. Eph. 2. 8–9; Tit. 3. 5; Rom. 3. 24; 2 Cor. 4. 7; 1. 9; 2 Tim. 2. 13.—Scott, *First Age of Christianity*, p. 193.—Royce, *Problem of Christianity*, I. pp. 265–6.—Von Hügel, *Selected Letters*, p. 193.—Heermann, "Ah, holy Jesus," tr. *Yattenden Hymnal.*—*Revised Prayer Book*, p. 112.

7. Eph. 4. 32; Lu. 6. 35; 1 Cor. 13. 4; Col. 3. 12; Tit. 3. 4.—Wordsworth, "Lines above Tintern Abbey."—Tennyson, "Queen Mary," Act IV. Sc. 1.—Sturge Moore, "Kindness."—Tennyson, "In Memoriam," CVI.—Hunter's Devotional Services, *Great Souls at Prayer*, p. 297.

8. Eph. 6. 6; 1 Cor. 4. 2; Lu. 16, 11; Acts 20. 24.—Church, *Spenser* (English Men of Letters), p. 151.—Young, *A Soldier to the Church*, p. 19.—Abraham Lincoln.—Wordsworth, "The Excursion," Book IX.—Hooper, "Life a Duty."—Sir Cecil Spring-Rice, "The Two Fatherlands."—X.

9. 1 Tim. 6. 12; 1. 18; 2 Tim. 2. 3–4; 4. 6–7; Rev. 2. 10.—Pringle-Pattison, *The Idea of God*, pp. 415–16 (adapted).—Buchan, *Poems, Scots and English*, pp. 84–5.—Wordsworth, "Character of the Happy Warrior."—Bishop How, "For all the Saints."

10. Heb. 12. 28–9; Eccl. 5. 2; Ps. 119. 161; 4. 4; Heb. 5. 7–8.—Spranger, *Lebensformen*, p. XII.—Whitehead, *Science in the Modern World*, p. 275.— Hocking, *Meaning of God in Human Experience*, pp. 473, 478 (adapted).— Von Hügel, *Selected Letters*, p. 51.—Rossetti, Sonnet 37, " The Choice."— Tennyson, " In Memoriam."

11. 1 Pet. 1. 3; Rom. 5. 2, 3–5; 15. 13; 2 Cor. 3. 12; Col. 1. 27; Tit. 1. 2; Heb. 6. 18–19.—Ottley, in Hastings' *Encyclopædia of Religion and Ethics*, VI. p. 779 (abbreviated).—Tennyson, " In Memoriam," LXXXV.— Tennyson, " The Two Voices."—Matthew Arnold, " The Scholar Gipsy." —Browning, Epilogue to " Asolando."—X.

12. Jno. 1. 14; Tit. 3. 4; 2 Cor. 5. 19.—Baillie, *Roots of Religion*, pp. 201–3 (abbreviated).—Streeter, *Reality*, p. 214.—Baillie, *Roots of Religion*, pp. 196–7 (abbreviated).—Eucken, *Problem of Human Life*, p. 144.—*Revised Prayer Book*, p. 123.

13. Jno. 3. 3; 2 Cor. 5. 17; 5. 15; Gal. 6. 15; Eph. 4. 23–4.—Middleton Murry, *Life of Jesus*, p. 134.—Eucken, *Problem of Human Life*, p. 133.—Hankey, *The Lord of all Good Life*, p. 331.—Masefield, *The Everlasting Mercy*, p. 67. —X.

14. Jno. 4. 14; Isa. 58. 11; Ps. 107. 35; Mt. 7. 7–8; Phil. 4. 11–12.—Thomas Aquinas, quoted Von Hügel, *The Mystical Element in Religion*, II. p. 152.— Hocking, *Human Nature and Its Remaking*, p. 236.—*New Sayings of Jesus*, from Oxyrhynchus.—Francis Thompson, " The Hound of Heaven."— Christina Rossetti, quoted *Great Souls at Prayer*, p. 28.

15. Jno. 8. 36; Gal. 5. 1; Jno. 8. 31–32; Rom. 8. 2.—Spranger, *Lebensformen*, p. 68.—Von Hügel, *Selected Letters*, p. 352.—Scott, *The Ethical Teaching of Jesus*, p. 117.—Russell Lowell.—X.

16. Jno. 14. 6; 1. 17; 18. 37.—Masefield, " Truth," in *Philip the King*.—Carlyle, *Heroes and Hero Worship*, Lecture II.—Whitehead, *Religion in the Making*, p. 5.—Nietzsche, *Ecce Homo*.—Emerson.—Streeter, *Reality*, p. XI. (adapted).—Milton, *Areopagitica*.—X.

17. Jno. 14. 23; Mt. 1. 23; 18. 20; 28. 20; Jno. 14. 16, 17.—George Macdonald, " Within and Without."—Hoyland, *Fourfold Sacrament*, p. 42.—*Sarum Primer*, 1558.

18. Jno. 15. 16; 1 Cor. 1. 9; 2 Tim. 2. 13; Rom. 11. 29; 1 Cor. 1. 27–9; Phil. 3. 12.—St. Bernard, quoted Von Hügel, *Essays and Addresses* (first series), p. 57.—*Ibid.*, p. XIII.—George Herbert, " Matins."—Henry Alford, quoted *Great Souls at Prayer*, p. 60.

19. Jno. 16. 33; Lu. 6. 22–3; Acts 5. 41; Rom. 5. 3; Jas. 1. 2; 2 Cor. 7. 4.— Wordsworth, " Character of the Happy Warrior."—Hoyland, *Fourfold Sacrament*, p. 89 (abbreviated).—Kropotkin, *Anarchist Morality*, pp. 27, 33.—X.

20. Jno. 17. 18; 20. 21; 4. 34.—Hocking, *Meaning of God in Human Experience*, pp. 510–11 (abbreviated).—Myers, *St. Paul*.—Hogg, *Redemption from this World*, pp. 224–5.—Browning.—X.

21. Jno. 18. 36; Rom. 12. 2; Mk. 8. 36; 2 Cor. 4. 18.—Von Hügel, *Mystical Element in Religion*, II. p. 360 (abbreviated).—Wernle, *Einführung in das theologische Studium*, p. 175.—Eucken, *Problem of Human Life*, pp. 164, 171. —*Book of Common Prayer*.

22. 1 Jno. 1. 2; 1 Cor. 13. 8; 1 Jno. 4. 8; Jno. 7. 17.—Middleton Murry, *Life of Jesus*, pp. 177–8 (abbreviated).—James, *Varieties of Religious Experience*, p. 489.—Ibsen, *Brand*.—Baillie, *Roots of Religion*, pp. 211, 218.—*Book of Common Prayer*.

23. 1 Jno. 2. 17; Ps. 103. 15–16.—Shakespeare, *The Tempest*, Act IV. Sc. 1.— Milton, "Lycidas."—Lamb, " New Year's Eve."—James, *Varieties of Religious Experience*, pp. 46–7 (abbreviated).—X.

24. 1 Jno. 2. 17; 1 Cor. 15. 53–7.—Way, *Letters of St. Paul*, 2 Cor. 5. 1, 4, 5.— Höffding, *Philosophy of Religion*, p. 206.—Shelley, " The Sensitive Plant." —Browning, " Abt Vogler."—X.—X.

25. 1 Jno. 4. 16; 4. 7–8; 4. 19; Rom. 8. 38–9.—Streeter, *Reality*, p. 210.—Baillie, *Roots of Religion*, pp. 172–3 (abbreviated).—Browning, "Saul."—Browning, " A Death in the Desert."—Wesley, " Come, O Thou Traveller Unknown." —Henry Alford, quoted *Great Souls at Prayer*, p. 54.

26. Heb. 11. 1; 11. 32-4.—Ward, *Realm of Ends*, pp. 415-16.—Kingsley, "The Day of the Lord."—Keats, "Endymion."—Henry Newbolt, "Sailing at Dawn," *Poems New and Old.*—X.

27. Heb. 11. 8.—Kipling, "The Explorer," *The Five Nations.*—Edward Everett Hale, "The Nameless Saints."—X.

28. Heb. 13, 20-1; Mt. 5. 48; Eph. 4. 13; Col. 1. 28.—Scott, *Ethical Teaching of Jesus*, p. 20 (abbreviated).—Jacks, *Religious Perplexities*, p. 103.—Ruskin, *Stones of Venice*, II. Chap. VI. (abbreviated).—Martineau, quoted *Great Souls at Prayer*, p. 69.

29. Ps. 23. 2, 3; 139. 24; 73. 24; 48. 14; Isa. 49. 10; Rev. 7. 17.—Shakespeare, *Hamlet*, Act V. Sc. 2.—Milton, Sonnet "On his being arrived at the Age of Twenty-three."—Newman—Charlotte Gilman, "Two Prayers," quoted *World's Great Religious Poetry*, p. 442.—Samuel Rutherford.—William Bright, quoted *Great Souls at Prayer*, p. 15.

30. Prov. 4. 18; Phil. 3. 12; Eph. 4. 13; Phil. 1. 9; Gal. 4. 19.—Graham Wallas, *The Art of Thought*, p. 49 (abbreviated).—Von Hügel, *Selected Letters*, pp. 90-1 (adapted).—L. W. Reese, *Songs of Praise*, 424.—X.

31. Rev. 7. 9, 10; Eph. 3. 18.—Te Deum Laudamus.—Bishop How, "For all the Saints."—Collect for All Saints Day.—Newbolt, "Clifton Chapel," *Poems New and Old.*—X.

INDEX OF SUBJECTS

Sunday

Monday

Tuesday

Wednesday

Thursday

Friday